RUBBER DUCK

RUBBER DUCK

by
Jack Douglas

G. P. Putnam's Sons • New York

Library of Congress Cataloging in Publication Data

Douglas, Jack, date.
  Rubber duck.

  1. Children—Management—Anecdotes, facetiae,
satire, etc. I. Title.
PN6231.C32D68   1979   818'.5'407   78-21247

ISBN 0-399-12176-5

To Mary Tyler Moore, who talked me down from the Golden Gate Bridge—and the Fairmont Hotel has *no room number 1326!*

RUBBER DUCK

CHAPTER

1

SEVENTEEN years ago one cold, clear, wonderful night, I brought Reiko home from the hospital. I eased her past the front hall closet and the two huge avocado plants which she had grown from their very own pits, and into our warm, wonderful Old New England living room in our warm, wonderful little saltbox home, in the warm, wonderful little village of Old New Litchridge, tucked away in the hills of the lower Berkshires, which at the moment, happened to be covered with eighteen inches of warm, wonderful snow.

I remember I handled Reiko like she was made of glass. Reiko, the tiny little Japanese mother of my first child.

I lowered her, gently, into our most comfortable chair, closed the front door, very quietly, and started to build a warm, wonderful fire in our enormous fireplace. As I sweated over the six-foot hard-maple logs, stacking them so they would burn at their most wonderful and warmest, I said to Reiko, pitching my voice at its most loving, and warm and wonderful. "Home at last, eh?"

Reiko said nothing.

9

"You don't *know* how *wonderful* and *warm* it makes everything to have you home again," I said. "My little Reiko, the little mother of my first child."

I kissed her on the forehead.

"Jack," Reiko said, ". . . the baby."

"Oh, yeah." I started to giggle like an apprentice idiot.

"Yeah, the baby." I opened the front door again.

"Come right in, Mrs. Ogelvie! This is *our* house!"

Mrs. Ogelvie, she was our new nurse, came in carrying the baby (which couldn't be seen, it was so swaddled in blue blankets). I smiled at Mrs. Ogelvie and tried to see the baby. I thought Mrs. Ogelvie swung it away from my view as she stood there and surveyed our living room. It was like Bismarck inspecting his new headquarters during the Franco-Prussian War and not approving of what he saw.

"This is our *living room!*" I said, for want of something really stupid to say.

Mrs. Ogelvie sniffed.

"We can put six-foot logs in our fireplace. We always wanted a big fireplace and now we have one." I smiled and continued toward disaster. "It gets cold up here in the country in the winter."

Mrs. Ogelvie spoke for the first time. "I had no idea it was so far from the city," she said. She made it sound like we had traveled for many light-years through space—passing Mars, Venus and Saturn—to arrive at Old New Litchridge, which was a mere eighty miles from the New York Lying-In Hospital, in a chauffeur-driven Carey Cadillac at one hundred and ten dollars plus tip.

"Not so *far,*" I said like a happy robin, "only an

10

hour and a half, and we love it up here—no noise, clear air, happy, friendly people . . . "

"Where's the baby's room?" Mrs. Ogelvie asked in the Prussian Field Marshal voice which brooked no familiarity or opposition, neither of which I felt she would get from Reiko or me from now on.

"Oh, yes," I said, "the baby's room. It's right up this *short* flight of stairs. It's *very short*." I started to lead the way. "It's all done in pink . . . the baby's room . . . "

"It's a boy," Mrs. Ogelvie said. Then, very reluctantly, I thought, she followed me up the very short flight of stairs.

"Yeah," I laughed, "hard to tell when you first start trying to have one." I laughed again. A little too hard. Mrs. Ogelvie fixed me with her cobra stare. "My things are in the car."

"Jack," Reiko called, as I stood there, not moving, "you'd better get Mrs. Ogelvie's things from the car."

"Oh, yeah." I was suddenly all action. "You feeling all right, dear?"

"I feel fine," Reiko said quietly, "just a little weak."

"I shouldn't wonder," I said. "That long ride from New York."

A snort was heard from Mrs. Ogelvie before she entered the baby's room. I kissed Reiko on the cheek. "I'll be right back." As I started for the front door, we heard the baby cry. I froze and Reiko tried to get up from her easy chair. We looked at each other. The baby cried again, and then again. I dashed for the telephone and dialed frantically. I thought the phone would never stop ringing on the other end. Finally a man answered.

"Doctor Rosemont? This is Jack Douglas. The baby . . . we just got home. The baby's crying and I think you'd better . . . "

"Hold it! Hold it!" the voice said. "This isn't Doctor Rosemont."

"Oh, my God," I said, "I've got to get ahold of him. My baby! Where is he at a time like this?"

"I don't know," the voice said. "There's no Doctor Rosemont here. You got the wrong . . . why don'tcha try the hospital, or the golf club."

"Golf club! It's the middle of winter. There's a foot and a half of snow out there!"

"Maybe he's only playing nine holes." The voice laughed and hung up.

The baby cried again.

"Maybe you'd better go and see what's wrong with the baby before you call the doctor," Reiko sensibly suggested.

"Yeah, it might only be a pin or something." I dashed up the short flight of stairs seven steps at a time. I opened the door to the baby's room, and before I could step inside, the door was slammed shut and I found myself outside.

"What's the matter?" Reiko called. "What's wrong?"

"I dunno," I said, hanging over the balcony. "Mrs. Ogelvie won't let me in. I opened the door and she slammed it right back—shut. I think she ordered me *out!*"

"*Ordered* you?" Reiko said, as I slunk back downstairs.

"Yeah. Je-*sus!* I haven't had anybody speak to me in *that* tone since I asked a civil question at the post office."

"What about the baby?"

"I dunno."

"Well," Reiko said. "Millie warned us. She told us how possessive these baby nurses become. Millie warned us . . ."

"Millie warns us about everything, including Ladybird Johnson."

The baby seemed to be quiet now and we started to relax just as Mrs. Ogelvie came out of the baby's room, gently pulled the door to, and tippy-toed over to the edge of the balcony.

"Now," Mrs. Ogelvie said in a voice that the Pope would have used if he had had to address the Easter crowd in St. Peter's Square without a microphone, "Where is *my* room?"

This question brought on a plethora of extreme silence which Mrs. Ogelvie interpreted correctly. "I see," she said, "I don't have a room of my *own?!*" I thought she was going to take off and leave right then and there, so I jumped in quickly.

"Mrs. Ogelvie, we can explain that. You see this isn't a very large house and well, we *do* plan to add another room but with the baby costing so much and the doctor and the other little odd items. One of these days . . . You see *this* house is the Mount Vernon model—ranch type of course, and, well, here at Old New Litchridge Acres, the architect's plans *do* call for an addition."

"Yes," Reiko added, "all we have to do is tear down the garage. Is the baby all right?"

"He's a very good architect though," I cut in. "He designed Bayshore Bungalows—that's a retirement village with tennis courts, bowling alleys, a pizzeria . . . bocci."

"He's designed a lot of developments here in Connecticut," Reiko took over, "Danbury Downs, Hartford Haciendas, and a lot of other wonderful places to live in Connecticut."

"You can have *our* bedroom, Mrs. Ogelvie. It's a lovely bedroom. I'm sure you'll like it. It's got a lovely view of our next door neighbor's rose garden, and in the morning when you wake up, the robins are singing all over the place and Reiko and I can sleep on the couch in the living room . . ."

Mrs. Ogelvie paid no attention to my magnanimous offer.

"How's the television reception way up here?"

She made Old New Litchridge sound like the heart of the Yukon.

"Oh, it's excellent," Reiko assured her, "isn't it, Jack?"

"Not bad," I said, "not bad at all. We do get a little interference on Channel 4, from Montreal, you know, NBC, but it isn't bad watching two programs at the same time—one in French."

"Where are my things?" Mrs. Ogelvie wanted to know.

"Oh, I am sorry, Mrs. Ogelvie, but when I heard the baby screaming in agony I forgot everything else. I'll get your things right now."

Mrs. Ogelvie, who must have weighed over 200 pounds, leaned a little on our balcony rail. I wondered about its tensile strength, but it held, as she almost snarled. "The baby was *not* screaming in agony. He was crying as any normal baby would. If they don't cry, they aren't healthy. Remember that!"

"Like 'All children have fits,' right?"

"What?"

"It was in a book written long ago called *The Egg and I*—a very funny book."

"I never *read* a *funny* book," Mrs. Ogelvie said.

"I'll get your things," I said, and mumbled to myself as I went out the front door, "If they don't cry, they aren't healthy. If they don't cry, they aren't healthy. All children have fits."

After I had left, Reiko told me that Mrs. Ogelvie looked slightly ominous as she clumped down the short flight of stairs and approached Reiko with a "we-got-ways-to-make-you-talk" attitude.

Reiko didn't know *what* to expect. She had never had the occasion to hire a baby-nurse before, and especially one who looked like Pancho Villa about to offer his prisoner a blindfold or a last cigarette— *either—not both.*

Reiko told me she smiled sweetly at Mrs. Ogelvie, but it availed her nothing.

"And now Mrs. . . . er" the baby-nurse had begun.

Reiko helped her out. "Mrs. . . . *er* . . . *Douglas.*"

"Yes. Mrs. Douglas. I presume you bought all the things I ordered so we may take care of the baby— *properly,* I mean."

"Oh yes," Reiko said, "I had Jack get everything on your list. He hates to shop, but anything for the *baby*. I've got your list right here." Reiko started sorting out her purse, which could have taken a lifetime, because she never threw anything away. Thankfully the list was near the top of the heap.

"Here it is, right here."

Mrs. Ogelvie took the list from Reiko's hand as if

15

she knew it could not have been anywhere near correct.

As I was hauling in Mrs. Ogelvie's luggage (which gave indication that she intended to stay for quite some years), Mrs. Ogelvie was going over the baby list with considerable "hmmmmmmmmmmming" and "tsking."

"The diaper service—did you call them?" she asked suddenly.

"I'm sure Jack did. I was in the hospital, remember?" Reiko said, with just a tinge of zing.

"I had a little trouble with the diaper service," I said, and saw immediately that this observation brought some sunshine into Mrs. Ogelvie's Prussian bosom. "I had trouble picking the right size. I didn't know what to say when the lady asked me. She said they come in four sizes—small, medium, large, and Here Comes the Showboat!"

"What?" Reiko said.

"I got 'medium.' I figured that would be about . . . "

Mrs. Ogelvie, not smiling: "Wrong size."

"Wrong size?" I said.

"Of course, it's the wrong size," Mrs. Ogelvie said, enjoying my ignorance. "You better call back and get the *large*."

"For such a *small* baby?" I said.

"Size, Mr. Douglas," Mrs. Ogelvie said, her lips were so thin as to be almost nonexistent, but nonetheless she experimented with a sneer, "has *nothing* to do with it!"

"Oh, really," I said, in a tone which was about half-

16

way between arrogance and Oliver Twist asking for more gruel (or whatever it was they were serving that day at the Orphans' Picnic), "what about 'Here Comes the Showboat'?"

"They were kidding you, Jack. They knew you didn't know anything about diapers," Reiko said.

"Well!" Now I was fuming. "That's a helluva thing to kid about! Diapers! I don't like that kind of kidding, where a man's family is concerned!" I took an overstuffed pillow from the couch and slammed it to the floor (not much of an effect to depict vexation, but it helped).

"'Here Comes the Showboat,'" Mrs. Ogelvie said, again with her no-lips sneer, "is for *twins*."

"Then the lady wasn't kidding!" I felt relieved. The tension which had been building ever since I collected Reiko at the hospital had been broken. I almost smiled. Then I told Reiko the good news. "Did you know we get a free picture of the baby with the diaper service?"

This revelation didn't set Reiko on fire.

"All we have to do," I continued, bubbling, "is use four hundred diapers a week for ten years."

"What?????" Reiko almost split her stitches.

"What the hell," I said. "After a couple of years we'll move. What are they gonna do—put the FBI on us for a lousy hundred and sixty-three thousand unused diapers? That's what it comes to."

Mrs. Ogelvie's tolerance for diaper talk had been long ago used up. "Let's check the rest of the list, shall we????" It was a command.

"Oh, yes," I said, not anxious for another border

17

incident which could lead to World War III, "the rest of the list." I reached back into the hall closet and brought forth a large unhandleable box.

"My goodness," Reiko said, "that's a big box. What's in there? The baby's crib?"

"The baby's crib is upstairs in his room," I said, "and he's in it. This is the sterilizer for the baby bottles."

"I thought it was for you," Reiko giggled.

"You're feeling better, aren't you, my dear," I said through my teeth.

Mrs. Ogelvie had been left out of this pleasant conversation too long. "Is that a Dandy-Steam Sterilizer?" she inquired coldly.

"No," I said, "this is a Blast-O-Mat. They didn't have a Dandy-Steam."

"Oh, well," Mrs. Ogelvie said resignedly, "I suppose we can exchange it. Where'd you get it, Western Auto?"

"You mean . . . " I was nonplussed. " . . . you mean . . . It *has* to be a Dandy-Steam, a Blast-O-Mat won't do?????"

"Not in *any* way!" I felt like punching her right in the mouth! (And this was only the first day.)

"Now, how about scales," Mrs. Ogelvie continued, a dedicated supply sergeant in the Green Berets, "did you get scales?"

"It was on the *list*, wasn't it?" I said, *not kindly*. Mrs. Ogelvie had spoken to me like I was a mental patient who had had to have his fly buttoned after he had just peed in his pants. I took another box from the hall closet, but before I had even begun to open it, she said, "You'll have to take 'em back."

18

"Jesus Christ!" I said. "Why? Do scales have to be a certain brand before they're the right ones? There must be thousands of different manufacturers, all making the same kind of scales!"

"True," Mrs. Ogelvie said. She had me. I could judge by her face. "But those are *bathroom* scales."

"What the hell difference does it matter where you weigh a goddamn baby? He doesn't know or care and neither do I!" I was screaming now.

"Jack," Reiko said, "Jack, you can take them back."

"Those are regular bathroom scales," Mrs. Ogelvie said. She was the only calm one in the room. "You can't weigh a baby on regular bathroom scales."

"These are the smallest they had!" I was still loud. "God Almighty, if I'd known a baby was gonna be this much trouble, I would have . . . " I stopped right in the middle. Both Reiko and Mrs. Ogelvie were staring at me.

"Why the hell didn't you put down *'baby* scales'?"

Mrs. Ogelvie ignored this. "Now, the baby's bottles. Of course, you got the *Duval* bottles with the *Fenneman* nipples?"

"If it's on the list, you can count on Jack, Mrs. Ogelvie. He got them."

Mrs. Ogelvie sniffed (almost sucking up a throw rug).

I was afraid to answer. It seemed that being a father was a lot more difficult than I had been led to believe, but I had to face up to it sooner or later.

"I *didn't* get the Duval bottles with the Fenneman nipples, I got the *Fenneman* bottles with the *Duval* nipples."

"Nothing to worry about," Mrs. Ogelvie said, al-

19

most, but not quite happily, "just so long as we have the Duval bottles with the Fenneman nipples in time . . . " She studied a gold watch which seemed to be on a yo-yo pinned to her double-ample chest " . . . for the next feeding."

"Now, wait a minute, Mrs. Ogelvie. Mr. Higby at the Village Drugstore told me definitely that they have never carried the Duval bottles with the Fenneman nipples. They only carry the Fenneman bottles with the Duval nipples. Besides, I don't see what the hell difference . . . "

"Mr. Douglas," Mrs. Ogelvie said in her best basic snake-charming tone, "it's not that important at the moment and I'm sure that Danbury can't be more than twenty, twenty-five miles from here. There are so many drugstores there, they're bound to have them in one of them. Just so long as we have them . . . "

"In time for the next feeding," I finished for her.

"Exactly."

"Oh, God!"

"It makes a big difference, Mr. Kirby."

"Douglas," I said. "That's the name I'm using now."

Mrs. Ogelvie continued right on. "The Duval bottles are much easier to clean and the Fenneman nipples have three holes instead of two."

"Well," I said, resigned, "I guess I'll have to hightail it over to Danbury and pick up a few three-holers."

"It won't take long," Reiko said.

"Oh, I know," I said. "I just never figured babies would be harder to raise than avocados."

"Now, Jack," Reiko said, "Mrs. Ogelvie's in charge

of our baby. We agreed to that. She knows what's best."

"I go along with that," I said.

"I've nursed over four hundred babies with my Fenneman nipples and I've *never* had a complaint!" Mrs. Ogelvie said, looking directly at me, daring me to comment on this last. I thought it over, but I couldn't say anything. It was too easy.

"I'll be back in an hour," I said and slammed out the back door, further weakening its already thread-hanging hinges.

Reiko told me that after I left, Mrs. Ogelvie started to fret. "It's just not going to work out," Mrs. Ogelvie had said. "Feeding time is in exactly thirty-five minutes."

"Oh, well," Reiko said, "a few minutes one way or the other."

Mrs. Ogelvie forced herself to be patient now. "Mrs. Kirland."

"Douglas."

"Mrs. Douglas, this is your first baby and you've put me in charge of it. So long as I am in charge of it, it will be fed on time! *Exactly* on time!"

Reiko told me she almost cried, but she managed to say, "But, Mrs. Ogelvie, it takes quite a while to get to Danbury. There's a lot of traffic right now."

Mrs. Ogelvie was not sympathetic with the world and its traffic or any other problems. "Mrs. Douglas, we should have had the correct Duval bottles and the correct Fenneman nipples here as ordered! Here and now—as they are needed! I run a tight ship, Mrs. Nickerson."

21

"Douglas," Reiko said.

"A tight ship!" Mrs. Ogelvie continued. "And I'm sure if we all understand each other, right from the beginning of the voyage, we'll reach home port safe and sound with no danger to our crew or our vessel."

Reiko told me later Mrs. Ogelvie had suddenly become Captain Bligh, and when Mrs. Ogelvie had left the room Reiko called her mother in Japan and told her what Mrs. Ogelvie had said about a *tight ship* and a *voyage* and reaching *home port* and would her mother come to Connecticut and help out? Her mother said she'd love to, but her sailing days were over and she had to stay home and watch the rice grow. Sayonara.

CHAPTER

2

IT WAS almost a week before we settled the Duval bottle–Fenneman nipple question and a few other problems about the tons of equipment needed to keep a baby healthy and happy.

We didn't see the baby at all during this period, and Mrs. Ogelvie was so busy tightening the ship she was going to run, we might just as well have been two pieces of useless furniture. I didn't think Reiko and I would ever get used to sleeping together on our living room couch, but with Mrs. Ogelvie solidly entrenched in our bedroom, we had no choice but to curse and enjoy it. We tried every position (including a few from the *Kama Sutra*) but nothing seemed to work. One of us always wound up on the floor curled around a bridge lamp and trying to pull the coffee table up over ourselves for warmth (an extremely difficult feat and a very unsatisfying source).

Thank God it was Saturday and too early for the ordeal of bed, so we were getting ready to spend an enjoyable—more or less—evening of television. Reiko was still a little sore and uncomfortable from giving birth, so I acted just like a regular Jimmy Stewart, plumping up soft cushions all around her. I was so damn attentive she said, "For Christ's sake, Jack, there's nothing crystal down there. Forget it. I'm fine."

This hurt my feelings somewhat. Maybe I *was* being overly solicitous, but never having had a baby myself, I had felt I could be empathic with Reiko and somehow know what a woman went through. This wasn't to be, so I said, "Okay. To hell with you and your sore ass."

"That's better," Reiko said. "What's on television?"

"Oh, this is a great night," I said, looking at *TV Guide*, "*The Untouchables, David Brinkley Reports, Armstrong Theatre, David Susskind's Open End.*"

The sound of Thompson machine-gun fire filled the room.

"Ahhh," Reiko said, "your favorite program, *The Untouchables.*"

"Right," I said, adjusting the sound with my little remote-control clicker. "It just started."

"Where's Frank Nitti?" Reiko asked.

"He'll be here, just wait. There he is now; the guy in the pinstriped suit."

"He always wears the same suit," Reiko said.

"So do I because I'm poor and humble," I said.

"You are about as humble as King George the Third."

"What is this?" I said. "What the hell do you know about King George the Third?"

"I found out about him in my citizenship class. We have to learn all about American history."

"Okay, forget it. Watch Frank Nitti, he's gonna blow somebody all to hell with that machine gun."

24

"How do you know?"

"Because if he *didn't* Bob Stack wouldn't have a good goddamn reason to chase him and that's what the goddamn whole Untouchables is about! *That's why* I know he's gonna blow hell outa somebody with that machine gun!"

"He did pretty well tonight, he took almost a whole bottle!"

Mrs. Ogelvie was standing on the stairs holding a half-filled bottle of formula. She had just come from the baby's room.

"What was that, Mrs. Ogelvie?" Reiko wanted to know.

"The baby, he took almost a whole bottle tonight!"

There was a very loud rattle of machine-gun fire as I clicked the TV up a bit. Reiko shouted into my ear, "The baby, he took almost a whole bottle tonight!"

"Every night the same thing!" I shouted. Then I screamed to the whole world, "HE TOOK ALMOST A WHOLE BOTTLE TONIGHT!!!!"

"Look," Mrs. Ogelvie said, waving the half-filled bottle above her head triumphantly like she had just won something in the 1812 Olympics.

"What's that stuff in the bottle?" I yelled back.

"Oh, they always leave a little."

"Yes," Reiko shrilled confidentially to me, "they always leave a little."

"How do *you* know?" I bellowed sweetly to Reiko, "That bottle looks a little *more* than *half-filled* to *me*!!!!!!" I turned the TV set down a few notches.

Mrs. Ogelvie continued at a half-shout now. "Yes, that's the one thing I pride myself on. I can always get my babies to eat. They really *stuff* themselves. Sort of a knack I guess. You either have it or you don't, and *I* have it! And when their little tummies are filled—poof!—they go right to sleep."

At this moment in time a loud, *very loud* crying baby was heard. The crying was coming from our baby, in our baby's room.

"I think the baby is crying," Reiko said, with everyday Oriental diplomacy.

"Maybe that's just his little tummy," I said. "Poof, the baby went right to sleep, but his little tummy is crying. He's a very tricky little baby."

"Let's not worry about it," Mrs. Ogelvie said as she settled herself in *my* easy chair, all set for an evening of television. "Just a little gas, he'll go right back to sleep."

The baby continued crying, and I thought, working himself up to maybe a bit of screaming-crying.

"He gets quite a lot of mileage on just a little gas, doesn't he?" I said.

Mrs. Ogelvie ignored this completely and snatched the *TV Guide* like it was the last copy ever to be issued.

The baby abruptly stopped crying.

Mrs. Ogelvie smirked to herself while I resisted a strong impulse to slap off her Pancho Villa mustache.

Mrs. Ogelvie settled back in my easy chair and adjusted it to its many positions so she got the ultimate in downy comfort. "Now," she said, "what's on the tube tonight?"

"We were watching *The Untouchables*," I said.

"Oh," Mrs. Ogelvie said, visibly shaken. "Don't you like Lawrence Welk?"

"We love Lawrence Welk," Reiko said, kicking me in the groin through ESP.

"*You* don't like *The Untouchables?*" I asked with a losing smile.

"Give me the TV clicker," Reiko commanded. I gave her the clicker, and in no time at all we were watching the Lennon sisters bleating their way through "On Top of Old Smoky."

Mrs. Ogelvie smirked again and I bled inwardly.

When "Smoky" had at long last ended, *there* was Lawrence Welk himself doing his Dutch Comic bit, announcing the next number. He explained (I think) that the next number was going to be "Home on the Range," as sung by, as he described them, "Our Two Lovebirds." (Lawrence certainly had a way with words.) The "Two Lovebirds" were in costume—one was a deer and one was an antelope, and when they sang "where the deer and the antelope play" they joined hands and circled each other just like real deer and antelope do. This effect was devastating on Mrs. Ogelvie; every time the Two Lovebirds sang this line she had an orgasm.

Along about the fifth chorus, Mrs. Ogelvie was a quivering lump of ecstasy and the baby cried again.

Reiko jumped up and headed for the stairs. "I'll go and see what's the . . . " That was as far as she got before Mrs. Ogelvie elbowed her aside. "No," Mrs. Ogelvie said, "I'll go, just to satisfy you there's nothing the matter—just a little gas." And she was up, up, and away and into the baby's room. Reiko stood, looking frustrated and bewildered.

"Come on down and relax," I said. "All babies have gas."

"Are you sure?" Reiko asked nervously.

"Sure," I said, "but we just happened to have a baby who could service a Zeppelin and have enough left

27

over to supply St. Louis for a week. Now sit down and enjoy." I clicked the television back to *The Untouchables.* Nitti and Bob Stack were shooting it out in a warehouse. With every shot, one or the other would put a hole in a beer barrel and what was supposed to look like beer spurted out. In three minutes flat that warehouse was a mess.

Mrs. Ogelvie was back. "Just a little gas," she said. "Whatever happened to Lawrence Welk?" Grimly, I clicked back to the Lennon Sisters.

The telephone started ringing. I let it ring.

"Why don't you answer the phone?" Reiko said.

"Who do we know that would call while *Lawrence Welk* is on?" I said. "It must be a wrong number."

"Answer the phone!" Reiko hissed.

"Hello," I said.

"Shhhhhhhh!" Mrs. Ogelvie shushed.

"Oh, for Chrissakes!" I mumbled to myself.

"This is Charlie Greeman," the phone said. "Jack, you having trouble at your house?"

"Oh, hello, Charlie," I said. "No, we're not having trouble at our house—yet."

"I hope you haven't forgotten, Jack," Charlie said. "It's our bowling night."

"Charlie," I said, "it may be bowling night over there—but here—it's *gas* night."

"What?"

"Shhhhhhh!" Mrs. Ogelvie was really up to full steam now with her shushing. "'The Indian Love Call' is next!!!!"

"Charlie," I said, "I gotta hang up now, 'The Indian Love Call' is next. I'll explain later—when I'm sane."

I hung up the phone and Reiko looked at me, her eyes a big question.

"That was Charlie Greeman. Tonight is my bowling night. You know, the big tournament—the Old New Litchridge Wildcats versus the A & P Gypsies."

"Well, why didn't you go?" Reiko stage-whispered. "Don't worry about us. We'll be all right."

"What kind of a guy do you think I am," I said. "Your first week home from the hospital, just after giving me a beautiful baby boy, I *think*. I don't want to go bowling, honest."

"'The Indian Love Call'!" Mrs. Ogelvie almost screamed.

"But, Jack," Reiko paid no heed to Mrs. Ogelvie this time, "it's the big tournament—you don't want the Wildcats to get beaten by the Gypsies, do you?"

Before I could answer, "The Indian Love Call" had come to its ear-piercing high-note finish and Mrs. Ogelvie turned to us and said icily, "Do you have a rectal thermometer?"

"I beg your pardon?" I said. I couldn't line up a rectal thermometer with anything in "The Indian Love Call" (which was still very fresh in all of our aural sensitivities).

"I said—" Mrs. Ogelvie was back commanding the troops, "do you have—a—*rectal thermometer?????*"

I had had enough (having lived through "The Indian Love Call"). "Isn't that," I said, "a rather *personal* question?"

Reiko pulled at my sleeve (like Jackie Cooper used to do when he wanted to get Wally Beery's attention in *The Champ*). Nobody remembers that except *me* and Jackie Cooper. "It was on the list for the baby, didn't you *get one?*"

"I got everything on the list, I'm sure," I said; then I had to know: "Wait a minute, Mrs. Ogelvie, what do

29

you want a thermometer for? Is the baby sick?"

Mrs. Ogelvie switched from Prussian commander to patient sufferer, "No, the baby isn't sick. It's just in case. It's something you *should* have in your emergency kit."

"Mrs. Ogelvie," I said, "if you're not telling us something . . . "

"I have a feeling you do *not* have a *rectal thermometer.*"

"I'll get one in the morning."

"Tomorrow's Sunday," Reiko said. "All the drugstores will be closed."

"You'd better get it tonight," Mrs. Ogelvie *more* than *suggested!*

"*Where* tonight? The drugstore in Old New Litchridge closed two hours ago. Old man Higby, he's the owner . . . " I explained to Mrs. Ogelvie, "is home sitting in his easy chair, guzzling beer and watching *The Untouchables!*"

"He *hates* Lawrence Welk," Reiko said.

"What about Danbury?" Mrs. Ogelvie said.

"Yeah, Jack," Reiko said, "what about Danbury?"

"You want me to take off now and go to Danbury?" I was incensed at this disruption of my whole way of life. "I might miss Gertrude and her Magic Violin!"

"Who's that?" Reiko and Mrs. Ogelvie both asked.

"I don't know, but I don't want to go to Danbury. I just don't want to go!"

"Why not?" Mrs. Ogelvie asked, in a somewhat softer vein.

"Well, for one thing [I was trying to think fast] they got a lot of hookers in Danbury and a lot of motels and one thing might lead to another and . . ."

"So long as you get the rectal thermometer," Mrs. Ogelvie said.

"But it's *Saturday* night!"

"So what?" Reiko said.

"All the *motels* will be *jammed!*"

CHAPTER

3

AFTER Lawrence Welk had said his *auf Wiedersehens*, Mrs. Ogelvie took off upstairs to our bedroom and I presume settled down in our nice, comfy king-size Hollywood bed and read herself to sleep with something by the Bronte sisters (which is better than Sominex).

With Mrs. Ogelvie out of our lives (if even for such a short break as overnight), Reiko and I sat cuddled on our bed-couch and tried to relax.

"Well," I said, "thank God she won't be here tomorrow."

"Why not?"

"It's her day off."

"Oh."

"I wonder what Attila the Hun did on his day off?" I said.

"Why do you wonder that?" Reiko said.

"Because I'm sure it would be the same thing she does, like go over to the zoo and hand the elephants *heated pennies*."

"I didn't realize how uncomfortable it would be with a stranger living in the house," Reiko said.

"He's not a stranger, he's *our* baby. Yours and mine!"

"I mean Mrs. Ogelvie!"

"I mean the *baby*! He's a stranger. We don't even know if we have the *right baby*! She keeps singing to him, '*Mammy's Little Baby Loves Shortnin' Bread*'!"

"Jack, I have an idea." Now we *were* in trouble! Reiko had been *thinking*. "I feel *pretty good*. Why don't we tell her we don't *need* her anymore? I'll take over."

We were in *deep* trouble. "Sweetheart," I said, "it's only been about a week since you got home. The doctor said it would be three or four weeks before you could take care of the baby. After all, there's a helluva lot to do."

"I'm not going to wear that white mask tomorrow!" Reiko said.

"Okay," I said.

"Every time I get anywhere near the baby she makes me put on that white mask. The poor baby, it must think it's a *stick-up* or something!"

"That mask is just to protect the baby against germs."

"I *know* what it's for, but why the hell doesn't *she* wear a mask. What is she— *sterile???*"

"I don't know, but offhand I would say that I don't believe that anyone ever tried to find out."

"Well, anyway, tomorrow I'm *not* wearing *any mask*!" Reiko said.

"Good for you," I said, pouring myself a glass of Julio and what's-his-name's best red wine. I drank it in one gulp and poured another.

"And you know," I said, "what *I'm not* doing tomorrow? I'm not going to *Danbury! Not once! Not once all day* am I going to *Danbury!*"

I took a long snort right out of the bottle this time. "God bless America!" I yelled. I yelled it three times and the baby started crying.

"You woke the baby," Reiko said. "The baby is crying."

"Well," I said happily, "that proves one thing."

"What's that?"

"He's still alive!"

The baby continued crying for least twenty minutes. Mrs. Ogelvie didn't leave her room to find out if there was anything wrong, and I had to control Reiko—forcibly.

"Take it easy," I said, like I used to soothe my horse when I was with the Seventh Cavalry at the Little Big Horn, surrounded by screaming red Indians (in one of my better dreams).

Reiko calmed down after a while (after the baby stopped bellowing) and we sat there, close, watching the dying embers of a $1.50 pressed-wood log. It was dying at the rate of about six cents every 2½ minutes. (I timed it one night.)

We were quiet and relaxed, it seemed, for hours when Reiko said, "Jack."

I had almost dozed off.

"Yes, dear."

"I'm worried."

Our brand-new antique grandfather clock bonged off twelve bongs, so we knew it was one o'clock.

"You're worried," I said, after the Seth Thomas interruption, "about what?"

"Well, you'll think it's silly, but I'm worried about tomorrow."

"Tomorrow's Sunday. You never worried about Sunday before. I always go down and get the New York *Times,* the *Daily News,* the Manchester *Guardian,* the New Orleans *Times-Picayune* and the Danbury *Times-Picayune.* What the hell is there to worry about, except finding time to read the goddamn things?"

"It's not that," Reiko said. "I'm worried about us being here all by ourselves."

"It'll be heaven," I said, and found myself another bottle of wine from our wine cellar, which just happened to be right behind a full set of Encyclopaedia Britannica and halfway across behind the Funk and Wagnall's Encyclopedia.

"But I'm worried. That little baby in that little room all day tomorrow with only *us two* to take care of him!" I thought she was going to cry. Now *I* was worried. My brave front was evaporating, even under the influence of my splendid wine cellar.

"Gee," I said, "I never thought of it that way, but we've got Doctor Spock's book, both in English and Japanese, in case the baby should sneeze or burp or— maybe have a bowel movement."

"Supposing he should *cough.* Then what?"

"Wait a minute," I said. "I'll look it up." I rushed to the bookcase, putting my foot through the glass top of a very poorly constructed coffee table on the way. Bleeding my way back to the couch clutching Doctor Spock, I started thumbing. Not before very long I came upon: "Cough: in adults, in the household 461, in asthma 477–479, in bronchitis 469, in colds

461–467, in croup 471, in measles 485–488, in sinusitis 472, in whooping cough 489–490. "My God!" I said. "They got a bigger selection than Sears! So let's not worry about him coughing, it's all right here in this book!"

This didn't satisfy Reiko one bit. "Maybe so," she said, "but if the baby coughs, how are we going to know *which* cough it is? What's the difference between a whooping cough and a measles cough?"

"I think that's fairly obvious," I said, slipping Doctor Spock back into his emergency niche next to my wine cellar. "A measles cough has got to be the one with the *spots*."

"Why do you always have to treat everything like it's a big joke?" Reiko said.

"I'm sorry," I said. "I know it's a big responsibility, but we'll make it."

"I'm scared," Reiko said. "Not for me but for the baby. Supposing I screw up his formula?"

"Oh, come on," I said. "How can you possibly screw up his formula? It's simple! Maltose. Dextrose. Water. And . . . er . . . something else."

"Like *what*?"

"Look, before Mrs. Ogelvie takes off for the zoo tomorrow morning, you get her to write it down. Maltose, Vitamin C, water, and whatever else goes into that concoction."

"Jack!" Reiko was in full panic now. "Jack, I *can't* do it! I *just can't*! I can't take care of the baby all by myself!" She started to get hysterical, so I slapped her and she slapped me back.

She obviously didn't know the rules.

36

"Look," I said, "there's nothing to it. What do you suppose people did before they had nurses?"

"I don't care *what* they did. You've got to go up there and ask her *not* to take her day off this first week!"

"It's one o'clock in the morning. Lawrence Welk has long gone," I said.

"What's that got to do with it?" Reiko was sobbing now.

"If I wake her up, she'll wanna watch television and there's nothing on but replays of *Lucy*. They're on all day and all night. Twenty-five hours. I don't know how they do it, but they do it. Look, Mrs. Ogelvie will be back on Monday."

"Jack, please!" Reiko pleaded. She was down on her knees clutching at my baggy Levis. It was like a scene from *The Drunkard*: "Daddy! Please come home with me!"

"Wait a minute, she'll be back *Monday!*"

"The baby might not *survive* till Monday!"

I never knew Reiko was capable of such emotion. Usually she was as inscrutable as all Orientals are supposed to be. But tonight it wasn't working out that way.

"Look," I said, "I'll help you."

"*You'll* help me?"

"Yes, I promise!"

"That's like being on the Lusitania and getting help from the Titanic!

"Those are *ships*," she added.

"I *know* what they are," I shouted, "but how the hell did *you* know?"

"I read about it, it was in all the Japanese newspapers: the Tokyo *Shimbum*, the Tokyo . . . "

"Never mind, look!" I picked up Doctor Spock's book again.

"It's *all* in *here*! This is the *Bible*!"

"Does it tell about *Jesus* in there?"

"Doctor Spock *is* Jesus!"

CHAPTER

4

REIKO and I discussed (fought) most of the night.

"Have you ever thought what would happen if the baby got the mumps, say tomorrow?" Reiko said.

"No, I don't think mumps are popular anymore."

"Well," Reiko, who knew she was winning, said, "mumps are still very much around, and if the baby gets the mumps, then just like *that, you* get the mumps—and you know what happens to a *man* who gets the mumps at *your age!*"

"That's an old wives' tale."

"Is it?"

"Yes."

"Did you ever read the life of Oscar Wilde?" Reiko asked.

"*He* had the mumps?"

"*All* the time."

Mrs. Ogelvie agreed *never* to take her Sundays off for an extra twenty-five dollars a week and a ten-speed racing bike.

CHAPTER

5

LIFE, as we were beginning to know it, was becoming an ordeal. Life with Mrs. Ogelvie, that is. She never left the house, and, as I worked at home and Reiko lived there, we were experiencing what could only be called terminal cabin fever. I had read about this kind of thing in stories by Jack London and others: two trappers spending the winter snowed-in in their cabin day after day until one of them goes berserk and murders the other. This was the condition we were living under. Very explosive.

Tonight was different for a few moments. Reiko was making a hooked rug which was in the same proportions of the Lakeside Golf Course. It would probably be the largest hooked rug extant.

I was sitting in my easy chair, taking advantage of Mrs. Ogelvie's non-presence for a short while.

"This is interesting," I said, flipping over a page in the *National Geographic*. "It says here that the Indian women in Peru often have babies while they are working in the fields and immediately afterwards get up and continue their plowing."

"What happens to the baby? Do they just leave it there, in a furrow?"

"Of course not. They wrap it in a blanket or an old shirt or something and put it under a tree in case it begins to rain, then at the end of the day they take it home."

"Only if it's raining, huh?" Reiko said. She looked pretty upset about the whole thing.

"It also says that Indian children never cry."

"How come?"

"It says they are taught from an early age that it is a sign of weakness."

Reiko laughed, but not really. "What are you reading—science fiction?"

"It's the *National Geographic.*" I held the magazine up so Reiko could see it. She didn't look.

"You don't doubt *them,* do you? Margaret Mead writes a lot of stuff for them."

"I don't like *any* of her recipes!"

"That's another Mead or maybe Sarah Lee—somebody else. And you know something, Reiko, darling, if a Japanese says something you believe it, but if an American or Greek or whatever, you doubt it. Why?"

Reiko threw off the enormous burden of her golf-course hooked rug and said, "Indian babies don't cry because they are taught that it is a sign of weakness. Doctor Spock says that a kid doesn't know what the hell you're talking about until he's at least three years old."

"Don't get sore," I said. "Maybe it means that Indian kids don't cry *after* three years old. That could be it. Here's something else that should interest you. It says that every fourth child born in this world is *Chinese!* How about that????"

"Must come as quite a surprise," Reiko said, "especially if the parents are Yugoslavian!" Then she laughed and laughed.

"Wait a minute," I said, "that's one of my old jokes from that album I made a long time ago. You know, the album that sold three copies?"

"That many?" Reiko said.

It was like old times for Reiko and me for a few more minutes, then the Fifth Horseman entered. She was waving a half-full bottle of formula like it was the Stanley Cup.

Mrs. Ogelvie, Reiko and I all said it together, *"He took almost a whole bottle tonight!!!!!"*

This was said without glee, joy, or celebration. It was said by rote, like we had all been programmed by Pavlov.

Mrs. Ogelvie was standing in the middle of the living room. She couldn't believe what she didn't see. Finally, "What'samatter? Television busted?"

"No," Reiko said, gently, "we just thought . . ."

Mrs. Ogelvie couldn't wait for any explanations, she simply clicked the set on. "Almost time for *The Untouchables,*" she alerted us with no uncertainty.

"Whatever happened to Lawrence Welk?" I said, knowing full well it was something catastrophic.

"He's on a different night now, back to back with *Sing Along With Mitch.*"

"Jesus! There's a parlay!"

"Yeah," Mrs. Ogelvie agreed, "Saturday night isn't the loneliest night in the week *anymore!*"

The sound of machine guns and what sounded like bazooka fire killed any chance of any further discussion of television schedules.

42

"Oh, dear me," Mrs. Ogelvie said, "it's already started!" She abruptly sat down on the other end of the couch, throwing Reiko and me toward the ceiling. With Mrs. Ogelvie's sudden movement, the couch had become a teeter-board. She didn't even look up to see if we landed safely. She just sat there staring at the television set and turning it up so it could be heard in Pittsburgh, Cleveland, and Albany. She swiveled the set so we could hardly see the picture. But she could see it just fine.

"Nice work, boys." It was Frank Nitti. "We wiped out the Northside gang. Now we're gonna take over the entire city."

"What about Elliot Ness?" another voice asked.

"Ness don't bother me none." It was Nitti's voice again. "He ain't got nothin' on me. From now on *I'm* runnin' this town and *don't you forget it!*"

"He won't," Reiko said.

"Shhhhhh!" from Mrs. Ogelvie.

"Now, [it was Nitti again] we gotta figure out some way to get that booze from Canada. How we gonna do it? It ain't gonna be easy."

"They're always trying to get booze in from Canada," I said. Mrs. Ogelvie glared.

"How about a pipeline, Frank? That oughta work?"

"A pipeline from Canada to Chicago! Are you nuts??????"

"He's nuts, all right," Reiko said.

Mrs. Ogelvie picked up a candlestick. I thought she was going to throw it, but she didn't, but she didn't put it down either. She just sat at the opposite end of the couch, toying with it, in case.

"I got a better idea," one of the shorter TV hood-

43

lums said. "Why don't we load the booze on trucks, mark the booze barrels MILK, and just drive across the border?"

"That's a very good idea, Little Augie," Nitti said. "But what about them border guards? Supposin' one of them border guards opens up one of them barrels and discovers it ain't milk? What then?"

"You pay 'em off," I said to Reiko.

"You pay 'em off," Little Augie said.

"Didn't I tell you," I said, cackling.

"Shhhhhhhhhhhhh!" Mrs. Ogelvie and Reiko said together. Now it was two against one. I sulked until the telephone rang. I was still sulking, so I didn't answer it.

"Mr. Douglas!" Mrs. Ogelvie ordered in her command-post voice, "the *phone! Answer* the *phone!*"

Murder welled in my heart, but I answered the phone.

"Hello," I said.

"Hello there," a jolly voice answered. "This is Lou Frogger of 32 Coachman's Lane, right here in Omaha."

"Omaha!" I yelled. "Omaha!" I yelled again.

"Yes," the jolly voice on the other end said, ignoring my astonishment completely, "I'd like to order a case of Cutty Sark and I'd like it delivered just as soon as. . . ."

"Wait," I said, "this isn't Omaha. This is Old New Litchridge, *Connecticut.*"

"Oh?" The voice wasn't so jolly now. "I don't suppose you—er—deliver?"

"No," I said, "but thanks anyway for asking." I hung up.

Reiko looked at me questioningly.

I explained, "Some poor dope from Omaha wanted to order a case of likker. Boy! Did he get a wrong number!"

Mrs. Ogelvie turned her glare on me and cranked it up to laser-beam intensity. I could feel my brain dissolving. The phone rang again. I picked it up quickly.

"We're all out of Cutty Sark. Oh? It's for *you,* Mrs. Ogelvie," I said, like a kindly water moccasin, and handed her the phone, which she took without a word or a glance.

"Hello. Oh, hello, Mrs. Randolf. Yes, I'm still here. Well, you know, we take the bad with the good."

Reiko bristled at this, and *I* picked up the candlestick.

Mrs. Ogelvie suddenly turned on me. "Would you mind," she said, her hand cupped over the mouthpiece, "turning down that goddamned television set. I can't hear a goddamned word!"

We turned down the goddamned television set.

"That's better," Mrs. Ogelvie said. "Mrs. Randolf? What? When will I be finished here? Oh, I guess I could cut it short about any time. It doesn't really matter. When is your daughter expecting? Oh? Well, there's time then. Yes, of course I'll let you know. Thank you for calling, Mrs. Randolf." Mrs. Ogelvie slammed down the phone and ordered the television turned up again.

I obeyed immediately just in time to find out why Bayer was better than any other aspirin which contained the same ingredients. Mrs. Ogelvie ordered the television turned down again while she explained.

"That was Mrs. Randolf who called. She has three of my children."

"*Your* children?" Reiko said.

45

"Not really." Mrs. Ogelvie smiled her vicious little smile. "That's what I call the babies I take care of." She sighed a long wistful sigh. "The Randolfs, they have *color* television."

"Good for them," I said.

"Yes," Mrs. Ogelvie agreed, "you can't imagine what a difference it makes watching the Weather Girl in color."

"I can imagine," I said, "seeing the weather in color. Here in Connecticut all we ever get is black and white weather. It's pretty monotonous. And how about Huntley and Brinkley and Bob Hope in color? Huntley's green, Brinkley's red, and Bob is plaid. Together they look like a rainbow that's been sick."

"I don't believe it!"

"That's why we don't have a color television set up here in Connecticut."

"Don't pay any attention to Jack, Mrs. Ogelvie, he's just pulling your leg." Reiko tried to steer the whole thing away from any danger of a Pier Six brawl.

Mrs. Ogelvie was still in a mellow mood from her phone call. "Mr. Randolf used to do the same thing." She sighed again. The memory was almost too much. Somehow the thought of Mr. Randolf seemed to have conjured up some sort of weird sexual fantasy in her latent libido.

"Mr. Randolf is president of the Randolf Packing Company. It's the biggest pet-food company in the country—Bow-Wow-Chow!"

"What?" I said.

"Bow-Wow-Chow!" Mrs. Ogelvie repeated. "Dogs Howl For It."

"I've seen those commercials," Reiko had to add. "Those dogs seem to love it."

46

"Oh they really do," Mrs. Ogelvie agreed whole-heartedly.

"They starve 'em for ten days first," I said.

"I beg your pardon?" Mrs. Ogelvie's mouth dropped open.

"I said that's the way they get those dogs in the television commercials to howl for Bow-Wow-Chow, they starve them for ten days before they shoot the commercial. By that time they'd howl for a bowl full of chopped chicken feathers!"

"Mr. Douglas," Mrs. Ogelvie said. She was working herself up into a cold-blooded riposte. "You don't know what you're talking about! Mr. Randolf loves dogs! He loves *cats*, too. And he loves pigeons and ducks and squirrels! He's always out in the park, feeding them!"

"How about his *wife?*" Reiko asked, feeling that she was being left out of what promised to be an interesting altercation.

"What *about* his wife?" Mrs. Ogelvie wanted to know.

"Does he feed *her* in the park?" *I* wanted to know.

Mrs. Ogelvie didn't jump at this bait. She ignored it completely.

"The Randolfs have a lovely apartment, the whole top floor of the Pierre Hotel. They have a maid, a cook, a butler, a chauffeur, and a cleaning woman!"

"How many footmen have they got?" I asked.

"Jack! Why?" Reiko said.

"I don't think they have any," Mrs. Ogelvie said softly, a slight tone of defeatism had crept into her former bold pronouncements.

"No footmen," I snorted. "Sounds like a pretty small-time operation."

47

"Is that so!" Mrs. Ogelvie was back on the track now. "As they just happen to live in the penthouse at the Pierre, they have a full-time gardener!" Ah, triumph at last!

"So *that's* how they do it," Reiko said.

"What do you mean?" Mrs. Ogelvie said, guardedly now.

"That's how they save money, they raise all their own vegetables!"

"I'm going to bed," Mrs. Ogelvie said, and clumped up the stairs, slamming the bedroom door.

"Maybe," Reiko said, "just maybe, the tide is turning."

"I doubt it," I said.

CHAPTER

6

MRS. OGELVIE was the Sado-Masoch version of the Old Man of the Sea. The moments Reiko and I had to ourselves appeared to be growing shorter and shorter.

"I don't know," I said.

"You don't know what?" Reiko said. She was now into crocheting what looked to me like Highway 66 from Albuquerque to Tucson, or else it was the longest necktie ever worn by Primo Carnera.

"I don't know if I can stand having Mrs. Ogelvie around any longer. If she comes in once more and says '*He took almost a whole bottle tonight!*', I'll slit her throat with a dull letter opener so it'll be slow and inhumanly painful."

"I'll help you," Reiko said. *This,* from the delicate flower of the Orient, surprised me.

"What are we going to do? We *need* her! And if anything *accidentally* happens to her, *somebody* is liable to miss her!"

"Like *who*?"

I couldn't answer that.

"Well, regardless," Reiko said "I think we can be thankful for one thing."

"Like what?"

"Like she agreed not to take Sundays off and leave me alone with the baby." Reiko shuddered.

"What about *next* Sunday?" I said, not to be unpleasant, but we *had* to face it. Mrs. Ogelvie had been hinting that she was about to break her promise about *not* taking Sundays off for the additional stipend she had been receiving.

"Oh, God!" Reiko said. "*Next Sunday!* She wants to take next Sunday off?????"

"Yeah."

"Ohhhhhhhhh!" Reiko started to howl like it was a full moon. "Why does every week have to have a Sunday in it? Doesn't anybody know how to *run* this *country*????"

"Look," I said, "you've got to face it sooner or . . ."

"Jack, I *can't* go *through* with it! I can't be left to take care of that tiny little baby *all by myself*!!! I know I can't take care of it! I'll do something wrong and *warp its whole life*!!!!!" She punctuated this with a *loud zonk* on a *huge Japanese gong* we had hanging next to the fireplace.

After the house stopped swaying, I said, "Honey, we've been through all this once before!" I tried to sound tough, but I knew that she was in a panic. *I* was nervous, too.

"Sooner or later *you* are going to have to take care of that baby, *all by yourself*!" Exactly the wrong thing to say. Reiko stiffened! She was in shock! Her eyes were wide open and did not blink. She didn't even see. She had become an instant zombie!

"Reiko, dear," I said, giving her a good solid smack

on all four cheeks, "I'll ask Mrs. Ogelvie to stay this Sunday. I'll pay her time and *half* or *double* or *triple* time or *whatever* she wants."

Reiko responded to this. Her eyes unglazed and her catatonia vanished and she returned to the land of the living. (Such as it is.)

"Maybe," Reiko said, always the Oriental pessimist, "maybe she won't stay. Maybe she'll want to visit her sister or the Museum of Natural History or something."

"He took almost a whole bottle tonight!" Mrs. Ogelvie was in the room, wildly waving the half-empty–half-full bottle. It was *another triumph!* God! Would they *never end*!!!!

I grabbed up a wine bottle and poured three goblets full and offered a toast, "To Hurricane Medusa! May it destroy *all* of *Miami Beach!*"

"What the hell does that mean?" Reiko asked.

"Who cares!" I said. *I* was hysterical!

Reiko got the idea and yelled, "Almost a whole bottle again tonight! Banzai!!!!!"

"Banzai!!!!!!" I repeated and snatched a souvenir samurai sword from its scabbard on the wall over the fireplace. I started waving it like I was annihilating hundreds of other samurai warriors with every slash and thrust. "Banzai!!!! Almost a whole bottle tonight! God has given us his most perfect gift and we are twice blessed."

"Twice blessed?" Reiko yelled and slugged a slug of good red California Burgundy. "Why twice blessed?"

"He has given us a baby who takes almost a whole

51

bottle *every time* and he has almost given us a baby nurse who *understands*!!!!!"

"Banzai!!!!!!!" Reiko yelled again. "Come on, Mrs. Ogelvie!"

Mrs. Ogelvie managed a small sip of wine and a weak, very weak "Banzai" and said, "What's on television tonight?"

"Anything," I said, " *anything you want!* Mrs. Ogelvie! The *night* is *yours!*" I couldn't have been drunk on one glass of wine, but I felt like I was *stoned.*

Mrs. Ogelvie looked at me with cynical eyes. She sensed that something was wrong, although she didn't know I had planned to kill her. Neither did I, at that moment.

"How about Captain Kangaroo," Mrs. Ogelvie said.

"Aha!" I said. "You tried to trick me on that one. Captain Kangaroo is on in the A.M., not the P.M.! How about the Channel 9 Super-movie—Rita Hayworth and Lex Barker in *Moon Over Mozambique? TV Guide* calls it a *ball-breaker!*"

"I wanna watch Captain Kangaroo!" Mrs. Ogelvie insisted in her best Ilse Koch manner.

I sprang to my feet. "Tell you what I'll do," I said. "I'll call that station, or better yet, I'll call Rita Hayworth."

"You *know* her," Mrs. Ogelvie was finally impressed.

"Jack knows everybody," Reiko said, which was true, but I didn't know Rita's latest phone number. "I'll call Captain Kangaroo, maybe she's with him." I started to dial.

"Shit," Mrs. Ogelvie said, and snapped on the television set. Then she rapidly clicked through a montage of underarm perspirants, cross-your-posterior girdles, Pepto-Bismol, and *My Three Sons.* On and on. And on. Mrs. Ogelvie grew grimmer and grimmer. Finally after she had spun the dial through all possible entertainment thrills, she clicked it off in disgust.

"Nothin'!" she said. "Nothin' but reruns and crap!"

"Would you," Reiko ventured timidly, "would you like to read a good book?" Mrs. Ogelvie looked at Reiko like she had suggested hemlock, which I felt wouldn't have been too much out of line.

"There hasn't been a good book since *Black Beauty!*" Mrs. Ogelvie snapped with Hitlerian finalism.

"I agree," Reiko said (I have no idea why). "But that's what I meant. Would you like to read *Black Beauty again? We* have a *copy* of it on our three-foot shelf."

"*Thank you,* but *no,*" Mrs. Ogelvie said. Mrs. Ogelvie's 'thank you' sounded like the next step was going to be a slap across the mouth with a wet leather glove and then a duel with chain saws (which *might* have been better than *Moon Over Mozambique)—far* better.

Mrs. Ogelvie did not flounce off to bed, as I thought she might have under the circumstances. She just threw her quarter-ton buttocks into my easy chair and settled down for an evening of baleful staring.

Reiko began to feel quite nervous and apprehensive after about fifteen minutes of this.

"Jack, why don't we take the dog for a walk?" she said. "I'm sure it'll be all right to leave the house for a while, and Mrs. Ogelvie will be here in case the baby cries."

"The baby won't cry," Mrs. Ogelvie said, with a junior snarl.

"And we don't have a dog," I said, practically.

"We could buy a dog," Reiko said. "There must be an all-night pet store open somewhere." Then to give credence to this. "They have all-night *liquor* stores."

"That's different," I said.

"Why?"

"Because," I said, "you can't drink a dog!"

"Jesus H. Christ!" Mrs. Ogelvie exploded. "Where's that copy of *Black Beauty?!*"

CHAPTER

7

MRS. OGELVIE stayed the next Sunday. And the Sunday after that. And the Sunday after that, all the while slowly changing from a kindly Prussian baby nurse who was only going to be with us for a few weeks until Reiko could handle the baby, to an antiseptic Mrs. Danvers with very little tolerance for the baby's parents.

"I wonder what he looks like?" Reiko said one day while I was trying to get down my all-natural breakfast.

"You wonder what *who* looks like?"

"The *baby*, he's almost *two months old!*"

"*Two* months *already!* It doesn't seem *possible*," I said.

"Our little baby!" Tears overflowed Reiko's beautiful eyes. "We haven't even had a chance to give him a name. Mrs. Ogelvie doesn't like *any* of the names *I* picked, the ones I *like!*"

"Well," I said, "we've got to put a stop to that!"

"How?" Reiko said. "I wanted to call the baby 'Bobby' or 'Timothy,' but Mrs. Ogelvie doesn't like either one of those names." Reiko was really crying now.

I tried to pacify her. "Don't worry about it, we'll call

the next one 'Bobby' or 'Timothy'. We'll just have to settle for calling this one 'The Baby' for now, anyway."

"But, Jack, he's growing up! He won't be a baby anymore. Soon he'll be going away to college or the army."

"At two months? I know they need volunteers, but I don't think . . ."

"I've never even felt his tiny little baby arms warm around my neck!"

This got to me. Suddenly and maybe a little late I realized what a terrible frustrating period Reiko was going through, but the change had taken place so gradually and subtly that none of us had been aware of it—Reiko, me, or Mrs. Ogelvie. Mrs. Ogelvie, who had genuinely loved every little newborn baby she had ever taken care of, had never stayed on anywhere as she had with us—and that's the way it had happened. Our baby had become hers. Reiko and I were the intruders, the interlopers who interfered with *her* mothering of *her* precious little baby.

Reiko, little by little, had foregone her madonna privileges, without knowing. The baby was kept in the nursery away from draughts, allergies, germs, and his mother (who was covered with germs from the world outside) and was still pressured by Mrs. Ogelvie to wear a face mask whenever she came within calling distance of her baby.

The baby, so far, had no idea who this strange masked creature, who was allowed to peek into his room twice a day, was. Reiko meant nothing to him. Warmth, comfort, satisfaction, and protection came

56

from the loving, omnipresent, cuddling arms of Mrs. Ogelvie.

The baby's mother was just the masked shadow. Gladys Ogelvie was his whole world.

Reiko was crying when I got home from one of my forced visits to the Big Apple. I felt like crying myself. The 5:15 out of Grand Central had run a few red lights around Mount Kisco, due to some miscalculation on the part of the eighty-six-year-old engineer, and had rammed into the rear of a parked tank car, which had been full but now floated in a large lake of No. 2 crude. Why the tank car was parked on the main line or why the rheumy-eyed engineer had run past the red lights hadn't been or wasn't likely to ever be explained by the rajahs of the railroad.

Explanations were too good for the common people.

It cost me forty dollars to take a cab from Katonah or some such way-station to our cozy little saltbox in Old New Litchridge, but it was worth it . . . until I got there.

Reiko's eyes were red and Mrs. Ogelvie was watching Lawrence Welk.

"It's nice to be home," I said, sorry that I had impulsively dismissed the cab.

Reiko clung to me like I was a handy log and she had just fallen out of a rubber boat running the rapids in the Snake River Canyon.

"I can see that you've had another happy day here at home," I said. "What now?"

"Mrs. Ogelvie takes the baby out for an airing every

57

day in the baby carriage and the carriage has a cover-all top in case of rain."

"I don't hear anything too unusual so far," I said. I was dog-tired, and very unsympathetic.

"She keeps the coverall top on the carriage pulled down till she gets a couple of blocks from the house, then she opens it up so the neighbors can see 'her' baby! Nobody believes it's mine. Nobody!"

"What'd they think that was in your belly for nine months?" I said.

"That fresh kid Norman Hagedorn next door tells everybody I'm a porpoise smuggler!" Reiko clung again. "He says I supply Jacques Cousteau!"

"I think we'd better move," Mrs. Ogelvie said one morning after her fourth cup of coffee and her fifth piece of Danish.

Reiko stopped trying to force the dishwasher to ingest more than its fair share of egg-sticky crockery. "What was that, Mrs. Ogelvie?"

"I said," repeated Mrs. Ogelvie impatiently, "we are going to have to move!"

"Move?" I said, coming up for air after a long draft of orange juice. "Move *where?*"

"Anywhere where the climate is more conducive to raising a child."

"What's the matter with the climate here? People have been raising children in Connecticut for over three hundred years!" I said (wondering why I even bothered to defend the Connecticut climate).

"*I* like it *here*," Reiko said, with a touch, just a touch, of defiance.

"Well, *I* don't," Mrs. Ogelvie said.

"I *still* like it," Reiko said, getting bolder.

The significance of Reiko's slight change of attitude did not escape Mrs. Ogelvie's experience with this sort of quasi-rebelliousness, and she lowered her voice somewhat, at the same time adding a contrapuntal leitmotif of ominous omniscience, "We will have to have a climate more suitable to the raising of children!"

I've never heard a tone quite so demoniacal, and so positive. From anyone.

She stood up and splashed the remains of her Danish pastry into her half-finished coffee, then turned and smiled at us like a rabid Mona Lisa and left the room.

"Jack," Reiko said, fairly successful in putting up a brave front, "I think . . . I think I'll take care of the baby now."

"Sundays, too?"

"Sundays, too."

"Good," I said, "I'll just fire her! I'll just go up to her and tell her, 'Mrs. Ogelvie, you are fired!'"

"Right now?"

"First chance I get."

"I thought so," Reiko said.

"I don't want to rush into this thing," I said. "This kind of operation takes finesse."

"I hope," Reiko said, "I just hope there won't be any trouble. She's getting more and more possessive of the baby every day. She frightens me. She's like some evil spirit."

"Look," I said, "this is America, we don't have evil spirits here. Mrs. Ogelvie is just another nutty nanny. We made the mistake of keeping her too long. She'll

59

forget all about our baby just as soon as she takes over some other unlucky couple's kid."

"Poor thing, she's so frustrated," Reiko said. "I wonder if Mrs. Ogelvie ever had a love affair?"

"With what?"

"You are wrong, Jack," Reiko said, as she sipped her after-dinner saké. "I don't think Mrs. Ogelvie will *ever* leave us and go to some other stranger's house!"

"She'll have to," I said. "I'll just tell her I can't pay her anymore—and we can't. This goddamn permanent nurse bit has cost us a fortune! We should have had the guts to get rid of her a long time ago!"

"That's easy to say," Reiko said. "*You'll* have to do it. I mean, *how* are we going to *tell her*?"

"We won't tell her. We'll just sell the television set and act like we never had one. If she asks about it, we'll just give her a blank stare and treat her like she's suddenly gone bananas."

"And that's just exactly what will happen if she hasn't got a television set. She'll go right out and buy one. God knows we've paid her enough money. She can get one of those new six-foot screens!"

"Well, why don't we try it? We can't go on this way!"

"That might have worked a couple of months ago," Reiko said, "but not now. Jack, listen to me. She will *not* go and *leave* the *baby*!"

"This is silly! She'll *have* to! What are you talking about? We don't need a nurse anymore, so she goes. It's that simple."

Reiko said nothing.

"I'm going to tell her right now!"

Reiko was still silent. She didn't look at me. Or anything. I walked to the foot of the stairs and called up, "Mrs. Ogelvie! I'd like to talk to you!" The door to the baby's room opened, and Mrs. Ogelvie walked sulkily over to the banister and looked down the stairwell. She was carrying a copy of *Black Beauty.*

"What do you want, Mr. Douglas? I'm reading to the baby."

I ignored this forced draft approach to my son's education and said, "Mrs. Ogelvie, would you mind coming down here for a moment. We'd like to talk to you. Mrs. Douglas and myself."

"Don't you want the baby to go to Harvard?" Mrs. Ogelvie said.

"Not particularly."

"Well, that's where he's going, or my name isn't Gladys Hermione Ogelvie!" Mrs. Ogelvie said, her eyes sending storm warnings to anyone who would deny her.

I had no inclination or desire or intention of picking a school for my son at that particular moment. "Anything you say, Mrs. Ogelvie," I said. "Now why don't you come on downstairs and we'll all have a nice cup of tea and—ah—discuss things."

"I'm sorry, Mr. Douglas," Mrs. Ogelvie said, "I cannot interrupt the baby's educational session for a coffee klatch."

"Tea," I said.

"No matter what," Mrs. Ogelvie said, turning away and schlepping back into the baby's room, closing the door meaningfully.

I returned to the living room. Reiko was still looking off into a void.

"Our baby's going to Harvard," I said. Reiko

61

roused herself when she heard this, and in a voice both confused and concerned, she said, "Oh, dear!"

"What's the matter with Harvard?"

"It's lovely," Reiko said, "but he's just a *baby*. He isn't even *toilet trained!*"

"So what?" I said. "If I know Harvard, they'll toilet train him in no time. They might even teach him how to read, enough to get through *Black Beauty* anyway."

"Jack," Reiko said solemnly, "we must not joke at a time like this. We have a problem. A serious problem. Mrs. Ogelvie will not *leave*, not *voluntarily*. We'll—we'll have to *throw her out*."

"My God!" I said. "I wouldn't want to try it. You ever see her do push-ups and knee bends, and she can chin herself fifty times without even breathing hard."

"She has to go," Reiko said, lighting a cigarette with a fluttery hand. "I *must* have my *baby*! I haven't been allowed to hold him for months now. He doesn't even know who I am and he doesn't care!"

"He doesn't know who I am either," I said. "How about a good stiff drink?" Reiko nodded her approval as I poured each of us half a tumbler of Chivas Regal from the portable bar, which had been a door prize at a Dean Martin Hunt Breakfast.

"A couple of little drinks like these," I said, "and we'll have Mrs. Ogelvie down here for a little conference."

"How are you gonna get her down here?" Reiko asked. "Right in the middle of the baby's cramming for Harvard?"

I splashed us another half-tumbler of Scotch.

"We'll tell her there's a telegram for her."

"Good idea."

"And just to make it legitimate, I'm really gonna send her a telegram."

"What's it going to say?"

"Dear Mrs. Ogelvie, you're fired."

"That's only five words. You've got five more."

"Okay, we'll say it twice. *Mrs. Ogelvie, you're fired—* twice."

"That oughta do it."

"Or maybe it should say *Mrs. Ogelvie, you're fired* and *love from all of us here at Sunnybrook Farm.*"

"That's - more - than - ten - words - pour - us - another - drink - Jack."

I poured another and another and another and in no time at all it was time for Reiko to crawl out from under the coffee table and make lunch, and I couldn't remember whether I had sent any telegrams.

CHAPTER

8

IT WAS late morning and Mrs. Ogelvie, when she appeared, gave no indication of having been fired via Western Union the night before. She just grunted and disappeared into the kitchen without a report on the baby, his bottle, or his bowels.

"Did you notice that grunt?" I asked Reiko. "She sounded like she was almost human."

"That's because she's taking the baby out shopping. She told me yesterday, she's gonna buy him some new toys. She says he's getting too old to play with that baby stuff *we* bought him!"

"What she gonna buy him, a Honda?"

"She's going to buy him whatever she wants!"

"Why don't you go shopping with her? He's your baby. Buy what you think he wants to play with!"

"I think I will," Reiko said, suddenly very gutsy. "I just think I will! He's *my* baby and I'm going to get him what *I* think he should play with!"

That night when I got off the impossible train at the mildewed Brewster station, Reiko threw herself at me from out of the darkness, sobbing bitterly.

"My God!" I said, "what's the matter? What happened? Baby sick?"

Reiko sobbed some more, this time very deep and poignant. She was on the verge, I felt, of a complete breakdown. Or wild hysterics.

She chose wild hysterics.

"She bought him a HONDA!!!!!" Reiko wailed. "A *HONNNNNNDAAAAAA*!!!!"

None of the other passengers on the 5:15 Run-For-The-Roses from Grand Central paid the slightest attention. As Reiko cut loose with another tormented banshee howl of pent-up dolor. This was old stuff to them.

"What are we gonna do? What are we gonna do?!" Reiko was ripping her soggy hanky to shreds and moaning.

She was hollow-eyed and without hope. I was more than a little shaken to see her like this. I didn't know that the situation had gone beyond *any* rationale. Reiko was now a very likely candidate for a wet sheet and a rubber room. And I was not too sure that I wouldn't be joining her if something wasn't done immediately.

I drove the dark, slippery curves of the rain-slick surface of Heigh-Ho Road very carefully. Not because of the slithery condition of the route but because I was *thinking*. Finally, after a long silence broken only by dry sobs of Reiko, I said, "I think I have the solution to our problem." Reiko said nothing.

"Don't you want to hear it?" I felt my tone becoming slightly edged (I had had four double martinis on the train). Reiko nodded dumbly.

"We've got to kill Mrs. Ogelvie." Reiko sat upright at this. I had piqued her curiosity considerably.

"*What?????*"

"We've got to kill Mrs. Ogelvie."

"But," she said reasonably, "what will the *agency* say?"

"They won't know about it."

"Jack, that would be *murder!*"

"And *how!*" I said, not without some trace of glee. "*Murder one!*"

"What's *that?*"

I pulled the car off the road and under the protecting shelter of a dying American elm. "Murder in the first degree—*premeditated* murder."

"Gee," Reiko said, dabbing at her eyes with what was left of her damp hanky, "if I'd known that having a baby would lead to murder, I think I would rather have had a chihuahua."

"That would be kind of embarrassing for me at the YMCA," I said, "introducing *My Son, the chihuahua.* I'd have to change my name to Dolores Del Rio."

"She's *beautiful.*" Reiko said.

This was typical of all of our serious discussions, they all wound up on a high note of disorientation.

I put the car in gear and drove out from under the dying elm and onto the ominous blacktop and home.

CHAPTER

9

MORE days, weeks, and months passed. The baby was almost ready for his first birthday party, and Mrs. Ogelvie was still shouting with great pride that *again* he had "taken almost a whole bottle!" What else he was eating was kept secret, although we did see tiny, mysterious empty jars of something in the garbage when we sneaked a precarious look. Precarious because Mrs. Ogelvie was *everywhere*, it seemed, and resented us checking our garbage. Mrs. Ogelvie resented us checking *anything* about the household. She had extended her domain far beyond just the baby and now reigned over the whole menage like a lord. Reiko and I were part of the fiefdom—*serfs* who were allowed to live there *only* if we knew and kept our place.

Our first and only child was almost a myth. We knew he was up there in the nursery and occasionally we would catch glimpses of him, all bundled up in the recesses of his Royal Coach baby carriage as it was wheeled quickly by us and out into the semi-fresh air of the Old New Litchridge park. The baby eyed us with great suspicion. This made Reiko cry and me furious.

"I asked Mr. Higby, the druggist, about arsenic today," I announced to Reiko one night after a delicious, wok-cooked dinner.

"Arsenic? For what?" Reiko wanted to know.

"I told Mr. Higby that we wanted to kill our baby nurse." \

"I'll bet he laughed. He knows that you won't even swat a fly or step on an ant."

"That's true, but I feel differently about baby nurses. I asked him if about three pounds of arsenic would do it? Mr. Higby said that he thought two pounds would be enough. He even suggested putting it into a bottle of ketchup and then inviting Mrs. Ogelvie to a hamburger cook-out."

"He's funny, that Mr. Higby, he goes right along with you, doesn't he?"

"Every time," I said. "I settled for ant poison. He said it would do the same thing, only quicker. I bought a gallon jug of *Uncle Ben's Organic Ant Poison,* no preservative in it—just pure organic poison."

Reiko didn't think this was too funny.

"What's the matter?" I said. "He knows I'm only kidding."

"Yeah, but Mr. Higby is pretty friendly with Chief Slocum, you know, the Old New Litchridge Police Department. Supposing he tells him about this some night when they're hoisting a few beers down at the Country Corner Pub?"

"Who cares," I said. "After all these years, I'm suddenly a *killer*?"

"You *look* like a killer."

"That may be, but if everybody who looked like a

killer was picked up by the cops . . . How about J. Edgar Hoover, don't tell me he doesn't look like a hit man for some gang!"

"Supposing Chief Slocum takes the whole thing seriously and starts asking you questions? What are you going to say. Why did you buy all that ant poison?"

"I'll be very forthright. I'll just tell him I want to kill our baby nurse!"

"That's crazy!" Reiko said.

"No, it isn't! You've got to learn, Reiko dear, if you're forthright you can get away with murder."

"How's your baby nurse?" Mr. Higby asked me late one Saturday afternoon as I sat on one of his shaky soda-fountain stools having my late-Saturday-afternoon malted.

"What do you mean?" I said.

"Is she still alive?"

"Sure, why shouldn't she be?"

"Last time I talked to you, you were gonna poison her with ant poison. Remember, you were gonna load a bottle of ketchup and invite her to have a few hamburgers."

"Oh, yeah," I said.

"I was telling Charlie Slocum about it, we were having a few beers down at the Country Corner Pub last night. He got a big charge out of it!"

Reiko had been right again.

"Well, she survived," I said. I had to go along now. "She's as strong as a bull—I think she could down a whole quart of ant poison and it wouldn't bother her a bit. She might need a few Tums for the tummy or something, but that's about all. She's a bull!"

69

"Gonna need something a little stronger. How about some bull poison?" Mr. Higby said, not wishing to drop the thing. It didn't take much to amuse him apparently.

"Got any other suggestions?" I asked, making disgusting noises with my straw on the last of my malted.

"Yeah," Mr. Higby said, chuckling fit to be tied. "Wanna borrow my Colt .45? I saved it from the Korean War. It's a lot stronger than ant poison. Quicker, too!" He chuckled again.

"What about . . . the blood?" I said. I still had to go along. Higby's was the only place in town where you could get a decent malted.

"What blood?"

"*What blood*????" I was nonplussed. "The blood from the bullet hole! Just like that old biddy to bleed all over our new living room carpeting. We just got it—wall to wall!"

"Well," Mr. Higby said, "I guess the .45 is out then. With a .45 it'd be blood—wall to wall. They make a hole you could drive a Pinto through if you had a mind to."

"I'd like to drive a Pinto *over* her."

"Better get something heavier," Mr. Higby said. "A Pinto will only give you a bad bruise. Know anybody with a General Sherman tank? They do a good job. Thorough, too."

"They got a Sherman tank out there on the green," I said, indicating the World War II veteran rusting into dusty memories in the middle of the Old New Litchridge green.

"No," Mr. Higby said. "No good, the kids need that tank."

70

"They let *kids* use that tank?" I was mildly surprised.

"Sure, It's Mayor Kincaid's idea. He says if the kids wanna express themselves, the best way to keep them happy is to let them do their thing."

"Oh?" I said, looking out through the overly Windexed window at the tank. "Somebody wrote 'Suck' and 'Fuck' all over that tank."

"Yeah," Mr. Higby said, "the kids. That's their thing—*art.*"

"I should have known," I said. "And I should be getting home. I gotta think."

"Let me know about your baby nurse!" Mr. Higby called after me.

"Yeah," I said. On my way to my parked station wagon I stopped to admire the suck-fuck tank. Down in one corner of its armor-plated gun turret someone had printed, "I'm a born-again Christian, but I liked it better before."

"Guess what?" Reiko said, after I had driven the wagon into the garage and bounced down the overhead door.

"The baby took almost a whole bottle," I said.

"How did you know?" Reiko said, without looking up from her roses, which she was spraying with just the *right* flavor for aphids. They loved every delicious spew. I didn't even bother to answer. I just flung myself down on the soft mat of expensive turf and lay there staring up at the darkening sky.

Inadvertently, Reiko sprayed me with the aphids' favorite nectar. It was quite tasty. Reiko didn't notice what she had done. So far as she was concerned I was just another rose. That suited me fine and I soon be-

71

came preoccupied with my unformed plans for the permanent good riddance of Mrs. Ogelvie. An enterprise which had begun to seem hopelessly futile.

I really had no thoughts of any real violence toward her, because bloodshed was not my forte. I had had enough of that in Korea. Up near the Chinese border I had killed a tadpole by accidentally drinking it in my morning coffee. True, it *had* given the coffee a certain delicate, almost erotic, ambrosial savoriness, but I've never forgotten nor forgiven myself, and every night since, before I go to sleep, I say a tiny prayer for that innocent little victim of war.

And maybe I'm playing it safe. Maybe God is a tadpole.

After a long, thoughtful pause, still staring at the twilight sky, I said, "Maybe." (My brain had become slightly more diabolic since Reiko had sprayed me as a rose.) "Maybe we could kidnap the baby."

Reiko stopped feeding the aphids.

"Kidnap our *own baby?*"

"Yeah."

"But," Reiko was unstrung by the idea, "what would we tell Mrs. Ogelvie?"

"Nothing. We'd just send her a note, made of pasted up newspaper letters demanding a half million dollars ransom."

"But she might *pay* it. She'd do anything to get the baby back!"

"Where the hell is Mrs. Ogelvie going to get a half million dollars?"

"From the A & P. If she stuck it up on a Saturday afternoon, she'd get *twice* that much."

"I can't picture that," I said. "Mrs. Ogelvie sticking up the A & P?"

"To get the baby back, she'd stick up Poland," Reiko said, getting back to her aphid catering.

"Well," I said, rolling my stomach into the cooling turf, "it looks like we're back to '*What are we gonna do?*' doesn't it?"

"Jack!" Reiko was suddenly fearful. She put aside her spray gun and her Green Thumb gloves and sat down beside my wilted body. "Suppose *Mrs. Ogelvie* kidnapped the baby? She *might*, you know, if she suspected we were sincere about getting her to leave."

"Yeah, and she wouldn't ask for ransom either."

"Do you think we ought to go to the police?"

"About *what*?" I said. "What the hell would we tell the police: 'we *think* our baby nurse is going to kidnap our baby?' They'd want some kind of proof and we have *nothing*! *We're* liable to get locked up in some funny farm somewhere until we got over our hallucinations."

"Maybe *we* could have *her* put into some sort of mental institution."

"Good thinking," I said, "but some *relative* has to sign the commitment papers, and so far the only relative we know of is her nephew, Clyde, and I don't think he'd cooperate."

"We could break his thumbs," Reiko said, making it sound like something that was done every day.

"Yeah (*anything* that sounded like *fun*), we could break his thumbs and smash both of his kneecaps with a baseball bat."

You think he'd cooperate after that?" Reiko said.

"I think I can say, without fear of contradiction," I

73

said, "that he *would,* but I'm quite sure he'd have to give up the cello."

I also think I can say, without fear of contradiction, that we were both high on aphid spray.

CHAPTER

10

THE baby's first birthday party was unique. His birthday cake had only one candle and the guest list had only one name: "Gladys Ogelvie." She played *pin the tail on the donkey* and won the prize. She made a wish, blew out the candle, and cut the cake. The baby wasn't allowed to eat his birthday cake, but he did have a birthday bottle of formula, of which he took almost the whole thing.

I was *allowed* to take some flash pictures of him being held by Mrs. Ogelvie, but when I suggested that maybe the baby's mother might hold him for a photo, the picture-taking period was cut short and Reiko and I were quickly shooed from the baby's room. So far as the baby's parents were concerned, the birthday party was *over!* I didn't even get a chance to give him the little rubber duck I had bought for him.

"But, Mrs. Ogelvie," I protested, as much as I dared, "I wanna give the baby his first rubber duck—I drove all the way to Westport to get it!"

"The baby doesn't *need* a *rubber duck!*" Mrs. Ogelvie

said, snatching it from my hands and tossing it out the
door and hustling us out after it.

That night at the Country Corner Pub I borrowed
Mr. Higby's Korean .45 Colt.

CHAPTER

11

"DOCTOR, why do I want to kill my baby's nurse?" I asked Dr. Hans Schaub, Old New Litchridge's only and very busy psychiatrist.

"You have a feeling of aggression," Doctor Schaub said, doodling a female breast in his notebook. It was a small female breast. The kind which would fill a champagne glass nicely, he thought, then he repeated, "You have a feeling of aggression."

"Doctor," I said, "I already *know that*! I don't have to pay fifty dollars an hour to learn that to want to kill my baby nurse comes from a feeling of aggression. I want to know what I can do about it? Do I have to actually kill her to get rid of this *feeling of aggression,* or is there some other way?"

Doctor Schaub finished his female-breast sketch and started on a tight little pair of female buttocks, with dimples, oh yes, with tantalizing dimples, enticing dimples, libidinous dimples. He said, "The feeling of aggression comes from somewhere deep in the psyche of the human thought process. The Roman soldiers in the third century B.C. had this feeling of aggression. That is why when they came upon a group of Sabine women bathing nude in the Po River they immediately raped them. You've seen the famous painting."

"Yes," I said, "but I don't want to rape Mrs. Ogelvie and I doubt that the horniest Roman soldier alive would want to rape Mrs. Ogelvie. She could bathe all day long in the nude, all summer long in the Po River and she wouldn't be molested by *anything*! Anything human, that is."

Doctor Schaub was now filling his sketch book with a huge object which could have been one of the guns of Navarone if it hadn't had a pair of testicles attached to it.

"Are you sure you don't have a hidden desire to have sexual relations with this . . . this woman?" Doctor Schaub said after a few more strokes with his felt-point.

"What woman?" I asked, becoming increasingly confused by the doctor's lengthy pauses and his apparent nonsequitur questioning.

"This woman you *secretly desire*!"

"Shit!" I said.

"Oh?" Doctor Schaub said, unnecessarily noting this in his book.

I spent two hundred dollars and four more hours with Doctor Schaub, then told him I'd "see him around." I felt this was the thing to do when my feeling of aggression was being turned from Mrs. Ogelvie to Doctor Schaub. For a few days I thought I might visit another psychiatrist to learn why I wanted to kill Doctor Schaub, but I discarded this mode of thinking as a prelude to a never-ending parade, marching from psychiatrist to psychiatrist searching for the answer to the never-ending question, "Why did I want

78

to kill my last psychiatrist?" I felt that this path led to madness, albeit a worthwhile madness, but I was not quite ready for this kind of trip.

Reiko told me that *her* psychiatrist was all for killing Mrs. Ogelvie.

"It will cleanse your soul," Doctor Farkas said, adjusting his pince-nez to a less raw spot on his overblown nose and doodling into his notebook. "You'll be reborn."

"But," protested Reiko, "what about the twelfth Amendment. You know: '*Thou shalt not kill?*'"

"Aha!" Doctor Farkas beamed. "Now we're getting somewhere!" Then remembering suddenly that Reiko was a $45 an hour patient and regretting his unpremeditated burst of enthusiasm, "I mean, this *might* be the key with which we can *eventually* (he made *this* sound like '*eventually*' and '*eternally*' were *one* and the *same*) unlock the secret room in your subconscious, bring your id out into the open where we may examine it carefully." Doctor Farkas made this last sound like the opening line in a porno movie. Doctor Farkas removed his pince-nez and rubbed some life back into the reddened depression in his unforgivable nose.

"My 'id'?" Reiko questioned. "What's *that*?"

"Your id, my dear," Doctor Farkas explained, with carefully rationed patience, which would shorten the time allotted to Reiko's mental problem, and lengthen Doctor Farkas's delphic orations, which amounted to little more than ethical time stalling, "your id," he repeated, "is that part of your psyche which is regarded by Doctor Freud *and* myself as the reservoir of your libido and your source of instinctive energy."

79

"I see," Reiko said.

My God! Doctor Farkas thought in a wild flash of panic. If she *understands* any of this, I'm in *big trouble!*

"In other words," Reiko said, "my id is dominated by the pleasure principle and impulsive wishing, and its impulses are controlled through the development of the ego and superego."

Doctor Farkas was in big trouble.

CHAPTER

12

IT WAS Sunday morning. I was trying to make myself as inconspicuous as possible in one corner of our living room. I wanted to read the *Sunday Times, The Sunday News,* and the *Sunday Newtown Bee* as peacefully and quietly and completely as was feasible in a house where peace, quiet, and solitude were qualities unknown since Stephen Foster had written *My Old Kentucky Home* there back in 1846. *That's* what the real-estate lady told us when we bought the place. And we *believed* her. Later we found out that it wasn't Stephen Foster but *Stevie Wonder,* and it wasn't *My Old Kentucky Home* but *It Must Be Jelly 'Cause Jam Don't Shake Like That* Stevie wrote there. Also, our house had been one of the Connecticut houses that George Washington had slept in but, again according to the real-estate lady, who needed a drink badly, this wasn't history. This had happened only a couple of weeks before we bought the place.

The telephone started to ring just as I started to get into *The Sunday News.* I usually don't answer the phone on Sundays, because if you don't get an early start on the Sunday papers you find yourself running over into Monday and sometimes Tuesday, but I picked up the phone anyway.

"Hello there," a semi-familiar jolly voice said. "This is Lou Frogger of 32 Coachman's Lane right here in Omaha, and I was wondering if that case of Cutty Sark I ordered quite some time ago might be on its way?"

"Oh," I said, "I remember now. Yeah, the feller from Omaha. It's Sunday here. What is it in Omaha?"

"You want me to look?" the jolly voice said.

"Well," I said, "it would be nice to know."

"Oh, I remember now," the jolly voice said. "It's Sunday here in Omaha, too. I suppose—just a coincidence."

"We don't deliver on Sunday," I said and hung up the phone. I'm a bastard on Sundays.

I had gotten halfway through *The Sunday News'* best feature, "*The Sunday News* Ghastly Crime of the Week," when Reiko came quietly into the living room. Too quietly.

"Jack," she said. I didn't even want to look up, I was enjoying "The Mad Butcher of South Philadelphia" too much.

"Jack," Reiko repeated. This time with a little more emphasis and a little less patience. "Jack—first the good news," she said.

"No games, please, Reiko," I said. "I just want to sit here and enjoy the murders of yesteryear."

"It's Mrs. Ogelvie," Reiko said.

"It's *always* Mrs. Ogelvie!" I said, flinging "The Mad Butcher" aside and looking at Reiko. She looked adorable with her blue-black hair piled in disarray on her head, her lovely brown eyes sparkling, but softly. I pulled her down into my lap and kissed her. She *was* cute!

"Jack—Mrs. Ogelvie is dead."

CHAPTER

13

"DEAD—*Dead!*" Mrs. Ogelvie???? I couldn't believe it!

"Very," Reiko said. "*Very.*"

"Reiko," I said, "—you didn't????"

"She was taking a bath," Reiko said.

"And you held her under water!" I said, aghast. "You drowned her!"

"Jack," Reiko said quietly, like we were talking about a bombing in Beirut. "Stop making a Lizzie Borden out of me."

"Lizzie used an axe," I said.

"I know what she used," Reiko said. "You made me read all about it in last Sunday's paper. We don't *have* an axe. We have a chain saw which I gave you for your birthday, which you have never even taken out of its case."

"How do you know she's dead?" I said, reaching for the nearest bottle, taking a long, deep slug. I started to choke. "That's the worst tasting Scotch I ever tasted!"

"She looks friendly," Reiko said. "And that's soy sauce."

"Where is she now?"

"She's right where I left her, right there in the bathtub."

"Maybe that's why I saw water trickling down the stairs."

"Yeah," Reiko said, "she left the water running. She must have had a heart seizure, right there in the bathtub."

"Oh my God!" I suddenly remembered. "How's the baby?"

"Fine—he took almost a whole bottle."

"Again!" I said, getting up from my easy chair (which I now had complete sovereignty over). "Might as well get started. Where's that chain saw?"

Reiko gasped, "*What*???"

"We certainly can't take her out of that bathtub in one piece," I said. "We got any empty cigar boxes?— or sandwich bags?"

"Jack!" Reiko said. "You're talking like a madman!"

"Of course I am," I said. "Let's face it, this isn't *The Waltons.*"

Reiko was at the phone. She had had enough. "How do you call the police?" she wanted to know.

"Dial nine hundred eleven," I said. "But forget it, they'll put you on hold for three hours. I timed it one day at the corner of 71st Street and Lexington Avenue. It was the time I got mugged. Besides, you can't call the police."

"How about my mother?" Reiko said.

"She know how to use a chain saw?"

"She's in Japan."

"Then forget her."

"Forget my mother!!!" Reiko was crushed.

"I meant," I said patiently, "forget your mother in connection with this murder. Why drag her into it?"

"What do you mean, murder??? Mrs. Ogelvie dropped dead in the bathtub!"

"*You* know that, and *I* know that, and *Mrs. Ogelvie* knows that, but nobody *else* knows that. So far as everybody in Old New Litchridge knows . . . Who do you think they are gonna arrest, who they gonna grill?"

"*You!*"

"*Us!*"

"What! You mean, the *both* of us? What about the baby?"

"What does the baby know? Are you kidding? He doesn't even know who *we* are!"

"Well, I don't know how anyone could suspect *me* of this terrible thing—but *you, you* were in the *Army* ! They taught *you* to *kill!*"

"Are you out of your mind? Taught me to kill? They taught me how to *stack toilet paper!* I was in charge of the PX at Camp Muckenfuss—or whatever they called that camp in New Jersey. They kept changing the name of the camp all the time so the enemy couldn't find our toilet paper."

"Who's gonna believe *that* story," Reiko said.

"*You're* the one who's in trouble," I said.

Reiko took a swig of soy sauce (*why* we didn't get a bottle of whiskey I don't know). "What does *that* mean?"

"You don't remember, do you?" I said. "Last Saturday night at the Dexters' party you kept saying you were thinking very seriously of taking Mrs. Ogelvie out into the country and burying her in a red anthill up to her neck."

"My God," Reiko flung herself on the couch. "*I* said *that?* I must have been drinking!"

"Oh—*that* you *were* all right! Then you said maybe the red ants would find her a little too tough to chew."

I wasn't drinking that much," Reiko replied, lighting two cigarettes at one time and smoking both of them.

"What about *you*," she said, "asking the druggist about all kinds of poisons, then borrowing his .45 Colt automatic?"

"They *all* know I was *kidding* about that! Besides, they're gonna do an autopsy, they won't find any poisons, any bullet holes."

Reiko laughed with absolutely no mirth, "Jack, you don't *know* these cops here in Old New Litchridge. They never miss *The Untouchables!*"

I thought I'd better change the subject. "Anyway," I said, "we've got our baby back. Now he's *all ours.*"

Reiko, always with the Oriental gloom (especially when the possibility of bluebirds seemed remote), said, "What about Sundays?"

"Don't worry about Sundays!" I said. I didn't need any extras in the anxiety department.

"I guess you're right," Reiko said, with infinite resignation. "We'll be in the Death House waiting to hear."

"From the baby?"

"From the governor. I never believed in those last-minute long-distance phone calls from the governor.

With all this talk about budget slashing, they're sure to be cutting down on those long-distance phone calls, especially to the Death House."

I couldn't believe that Reiko had given up all hope on what seemed to me to be a very simple problem— or no problem at all—if we used our heads.

"We're just going to have to get rid of Mrs. Ogelvie," I said.

"But," Reiko protested, "you said we haven't done anything."

"We haven't," I said, "but can't you just see those headlines in the New York Papers? PROMINENT CONNECTICUT JET-SETTERS' NURSE FOUND DEAD—POLICE REPORT IMMINENT ARRESTS.

"*Who* are the *prominent Connecticut Jet-Setters?*"

"*We* are. Anybody who lives anywhere near an approach runway to JFK, according to the *Daily News*, is a jet-setter."

"This whole thing is silly, we've got to call the police. Maybe Mrs. Ogelvie just slipped in the bathtub. She's lying there. That's the way I found her, just lying there on her back with a nasty bruise on her forehead."

This, I didn't like. I waited for a moment before I spoke. "She's lying there on her *back* with a *nasty bruise* on her *forehead?*"

Reiko looked at me, puzzled. "What's the matter?"

"Just one thing, *one little thing*, *how* did she get the nasty bruise on her forehead?"

"She must have bumped it on something when she slipped and fell down in the bathtub. How else?"

"*Bumped* it? On *what?*" I was Inspector Flannagan of Scotland Yard now.

"How should *I* know?" Reiko was fed up with the whole thing by this time, and scared. So was I.

"Or," I continued, "she may have been hit on the head with a blunt instrument that started her on her way down."

"*What* blunt instrument?" Reiko said sardonically. "A Waterpik?"

"How about a frozen leg of lamb? Do you happen to have a frozen leg of lamb in the freezer?"

"I happen to have *several* frozen legs of lamb in the freezer."

"I rest my case," I said.

"What in the hell are you *talking* about?" Reiko said.

"You zonked Mrs. Ogelvie on the head with this frozen leg of lamb, crushing her skull, then you put this blunt instrument back in the deep freeze and the police will never find the murder weapon. Isn't *that* the way it *happened*?"

"Jack, I read that same story in the *Reader's Digest* or wherever. *Everybody* has read that story a *zillion times*, it's been printed in every adventure magazine all over the world! Besides, why are you trying to hang this thing on me?"

"You wouldn't want to see ME mixed up in this, would you?"

"Now that you mention it," Reiko said, "why not?"

I think the relief of knowing that Mrs. Ogelvie was gone, for good, was making us both a little giddy.

"Look, no matter what happened, the police are going to ask us questions. Embarrasssing questions. And we better have some pretty good answers. On the other hand, if she just *disappears* and *they* or *nobody else*

89

can *find* her, we're home free! *We* know we didn't do anything!"

"How am I going to explain my suddenly appearing with a baby in my arms that nobody knows is *mine!*"

"You don't have to explain. Or if somebody asks you, just say it's a munchkin and it just followed you home from the *Wizard of Oz*, or don't bother to say anything. Our big problem now is *getting rid* of *Mrs. Ogelvie!*"

Reiko agreed with this and I started to ponder. "No, we'd never get it into the house or even in the yard."

"What are you talking about now?"

"I was thinking," I said, "about those guys in the circus—the Zacchini's or whatever their name is—they shoot each other out of a great big cannon. I used to know one of the Zacchinis—Hugo—if we could just borrow his cannon some night and shoot Mrs. Ogelvie into that big swamp over by Mud Pond, nobody ever goes there except for a few bird-watchers."

"There's your trouble," Reiko said, "bird-watchers—they may think it's a fat flamingo with a feather problem and report it."

"I'm just raving on," I said. "In the first place, I don't know how we could carry her out of here, even if we had a place to dump her. She must weigh at least . . ."

"How about the chain saw?" Reiko tried to smile.

"You're kidding," I said. "I've never dissected anything but a frog, and that was in biology in high school, and even then I couldn't do it. I let the frog es-

90

cape. I had to flush three times before that dopey frog got the idea."

We both sat there, thinking and drinking (we finally had become aware enough to switch from soy sauce to Chivas Regal, which is the soy sauce of royalty—in Peking, anyway).

"One thing I think we're going to need," Reiko said, and very practically, too, "is a trunk, a very large, well-constructed trunk."

"You're absolutely right," I agreed wholeheartedly. "But where, where are we gonna get a trunk on a *Sunday*? This is Sunday. We gonna get a trunk at church? All *they* have on Sunday is *wine* and *wafers* and some very practical advice on adultery. They make it sound like a helluva lot of fun and it is."

Reiko ignored this completely because she had no idea of what I was speaking. "Tonight," she said, "they're having a church supper and an auction and Bingo."

"I love Bingo," I said. "I wish I had been Catholic instead of Episcopalian. All *we* have is craps—with round dice."

"Tonight they're trying to collect enough money to give Father Meech a raise."

"What?"

"Yes, Father Meech is threatening a job action— dragging out the service to two hours instead of one. And no contributions you can't fold."

"I don't understand," I said.

"He's been threatening this ever since the insurance company raised his malpractice rate. Father Meech says he can't risk the wrath of God and All-state, too."

"Do you think maybe the auction," I said. "Maybe somebody'll want to get rid of a large trunk or maybe a piano case. That would be better. Anyway, the auction sounds like a good idea. Oh my God! We need a sitter—a babysitter—now that Mrs Ogelvie's . . ."

"Don't worry," Reiko said. "I'll take care of that."

"But," I said, "supposing she wants to go to the bathroom—the sitter? We only have *one bathroom*, you know."

"I'll take care of that, too." Reiko said. "Get that moosehead we've got hanging over the fireplace."

"The moosehead? I *love* that moosehead. Just because it's a little cross-eyed *you* never . . . what are you going to do with my favorite cross-eyed moose?"

"I'm not going to hurt it anyway," Reiko said. "All I'm going to do is hang it on the wall in the bathroom facing the door, then I'm going to put a sign on the outside of the door: *BEWARE OF THE MOOSE!*"

"You think that's gonna keep her out of the bathroom?"

"No, but it'll keep her from staying in there. No nice girl is gonna drop her drawers in the same room with a cross-eyed moose!"

"I suppose that's true," I said, not entirely convinced.

CHAPTER

14

"WHERE the hell is the babysitter?" I said. "It's eight o'clock. Wasn't she supposed to be here at eight?"

"Relax," Reiko said. "You know these high school kids, they're not always exactly on time. And for three dollars an hour you can't expect too much."

"Three dollars an hour for a babysitter! You can get an armed guard from Brinks for five!"

"That was back in the days of the buffalo," Reiko said, just as some kind of hopped-up car made a screaming turn into our driveway and two car doors slammed almost simultaneously.

"Here they are," Reiko said, and turned to open the front door.

"They?" I said.

Reiko opened the door and a beautiful young girl about eighteen years old bubbled her way into the house, followed by a seven-foot-three lout wearing a ragged school sweater, torn jeans, and scuffed-beyond-redemption sneakers—no sox.

"I'm Debbie Braunsweig and this"—pointing to the lout—"is 'Jumpy' Campbell. They call him 'Jumpy' because he jumps center on the basketball team. He's terrific!" Debbie bubbled a little more.

"He's . . . er . . . 'Jumpy' is gonna sit with you?" I asked superfluously.

"Yeah," Debbie said, "and that's all. No funny stuff. You don't hafta worry about any funny stuff unless you're gonna be late."

"You can't use the bathroom," Reiko said, abruptly, I thought.

This stopped Debbie's bubbling for a moment, "Er . . . why?" Then she gestured toward "Jumpy." "He's okay. He knows how."

"No, no," I explained. "What Mrs. Douglas means is that we have a plumbing problem. We have to use the filling station down at the corner, the Esso station."

"Where's the brat?" Debbie wanted to know now that the bathroom problem had been solved.

"Brat?" Reiko said. "Oh, the *baby*."

"Now you got it," Debbie said. Debbie treated Reiko like she just got to America fresh from a Japanese rice field. "Yeah, baby."

"He's in his little room," Reiko said, lighting a cigarette, as she always did when she was nervous about something, "in his little crib. He took almost a whole bottle tonight."

"Jumpy" was suddenly alert. "A whole bottle of what?"

"Jumpy," Debbie said, "forget it! You wouldn't like it!"

"Jumpy" was crushed. "Why does everybody always say, 'I wouldn't like it?' There's a lotta things I like. I

94

like vodka, vodka over bourbon, straight, no ice. I like . . ."

"Later, Jumpy," Debbie said, "later. Have a nice time at the church supper, Mr. and Mrs. Douglas." She ushered us out the front door, "And don't, for God's sake, don't eat the *potato salad!*"

"Why not?" I said.

"Because," Debbie said, "my mother made it and she accidentally dropped most of it on the kitchen floor and the dog chased the cat through it a few times before she could scoop it up and put it back in the bowl."

"I'm glad you told us," I said, helping Reiko into her Hudson Bay jacket. "And remember, don't forget the toilet."

"How could I?" Debbie said.

We were barreling down Elm Street toward the church when I heard the police siren and saw the flashing red light right up behind us.

I stopped the car immediately and put my hands on top of my head, the way they had taught me in California a few years before so as to avoid the unforgettable experience of getting shot first and questioned afterward. This I learned from my then next-door neighbor in Hollywood, who happened to be a member of the California Highway Patrol.

The cop got out of his car and strolled up to the driver's side. It was Officer Sandy Powell. "Okay, Jack," Sandy said, "let's not have any dramatics. This isn't *Dragnet.* You can put your hands down."

"Sorry, Sandy," I said, "just habit."

Immediately Sandy, who was a very alert police officer, said, "You been arrested before?"

"Only for rape," I said. "This little eighty-seven-year-old lady was thumbing a ride and I stopped and . . ."

"Hey," Sandy said, leaning his head inside the car, "I wanna ask you—did you finally knock off your baby's nurse?"

Christ! I thought, did our babysitter discover Mrs. Ogelvie in the bathtub and call the cops? I really felt I had to play it straight now.

"But how did you know, Sandy? Did it come over the old 10-4?"

"We been laughin' about that around the station-house ever since old man Higby, the druggist, told us. Jesus, Jack. You ever shoot a .45?"

"Well, no," I said, "not exactly. I had one in the Army, but in our platoon they were afraid to give us ammo. They said they had enough to worry about with the Krauts in *front* of them. They didn't want to get their butts shot off at the same time!"

Sandy and I had a good laugh about this old Army bullshit, and Reiko, not understanding, laughed along, somewhat.

"Well," Sandy said, "let me warn you, Jack. Don't knock off that old lady with a .45. Use something smaller, or better still, just whack her over the head with something heavy and deadly like a frozen leg of lamb. You ever read that story in the *Reader's Digest*— funny story, the perfect crime. She put the frozen leg of lamb back in the deep freezer and nobody ever found the weapon that knocked off her husband."

Reiko finally spoke up. "Whose husband?"

96

"The dame who bashed her husband on the head with the frozen leg of lamb," Sandy said. "If I find that old copy of the *Reader's Digest*, I'll keep it for you—funny story."

"Would you do that, Sandy?" I said.

"Sure and, Jack, please get your tail-lights fixed, will you? It's been two years now. See you later."

Sandy went back to his prowl car and Reiko and I waited until he had pulled away. We both heaved heavy sighs of relief. I could see now why murder is such a specialized profession—you had to have just the right kind of highly tuned nerves. People like us were just no damn good at it and never would be.

We were lucky at the church supper and auction. We didn't eat the potato salad and we bought an enormous trunk. It looked like the kind of trunk that Houdini, the great magician, would have used in his act. It was big enough to contain a very large human being, which of course was perfect for us, the Old New Litchridge body shippers.

It took us almost half an hour to get it tied to the top of our smallish station wagon with the help of a lot of rope and a couple of boys in the choir who had been smoking a little grass in the parking lot. When we finally got this enormous trunk in place, I felt we shouldn't try to make it under any low bridges, so I chose a roundabout way to go home. We passed Sandy in his prowl car twice, which didn't build our morale at all.

At last, we swung into our driveway and straight into our open-doored garage. This was a mistake. What we had left when it was all over—with the tremendous crash of the trunk hitting the top of the garage opening and the ripping off of our station wagon luggage rack—was a nice little station wagon all snug in its own cozy garage . . . and a very large trunk embedded in the outside wall. (Somewhere in the back of the trunk, crushed into a shapelessness beyond recognition, was a basketball hoop.) Needless to say, this gaffe did not go unnoticed by anyone for miles around. In our immediate neighborhood fifty windows were flung open simultaneously. Lights outside and inside were turned on, transforming night into day just like that.

Reiko and I sat in the car for a long moment, afraid to investigate our latest disaster. Finally we had no choice. We were surrounded by ghouls in various stages of dress and undress. Hair in curlers, one eyelash on, one off, some of the men who had been shaving were covered with lather and no little blood. There were bare feet and slippers. It seemed we had timed it just right for the bedtime hour, or as it was known on our street, *Johnny Carson Time*, which could mean anything from "Let's watch the show" to "How about it, honey?"

Any plans that anyone may have had for television, reading or fornicating or just plain sleeping had been shot by our eruptive arrival home.

There were so many "What happened, Jacks?" and "Reiko, are you all right?" I felt I should explain. "Okay," I said, "which one of you wise apples tried to throw that trunk into our basketball hoop? And just for that there'll be no game next Saturday!"

There was a series of blank looks exchanged all around.

At that moment the trunk chose to become unstuck from the garage wall and came crashing down onto the driveway, narrowly missing everybody.

The neighbors, one and all, started edging away from us. In no time at all we were alone.

The front of the garage at the impact point was damaged to a high degree, but the trunk hadn't been scratched. We had really bought ourselves a sturdy piece of goods.

At that moment, a little late I thought, Debbie and her boyfriend Jumpy arrived outside. "What's going on out here?" Debbie said.

"What was going on in there?" I countered. "How's the baby?"

"What baby? Oh, *your* baby. He's fine and we didn't use the bathroom. Jumpy here had to go, but, well, he figured he couldn't make it all the way to the filling station so he . . . he went out back."

"Look at my rose bushes," Reiko said. "They're *all* flat!"

"Yeah," Jumpy said, "I really had to *go!*"

CHAPTER

15

MRS. OGELVIE was not a pretty sight, lying there in the bathtub. She had never been a pretty sight alive. But, now she had gone and overdone it. Nonetheless, we had committed ourselves and we had no choice.

Two hours and thirty-six minutes later we had her sitting inside the trunk we had bought at the church auction, down the stairs, and placed in the middle of our living room, where our coffee table used to be.

"How the hell did we do it?" I asked of no one in particular. The combined weight of the trunk and Mrs. Ogelvie must have been pretty close to the combined weight of a loaded Liberian tanker.

"Now what?" Reiko said, lying on the couch dripping with sweat and aching in every muscle, or so she told me—many times.

"I wish," I said softly, very softly because I was two steps ahead of collapse or two steps behind, "I wish I had read more detective stories, like all that Agatha Christie stuff. I'm sure I could remember something in one of those stories that would help us now. How do you get rid of a two-hundred-pound nurse in a hundred-pound trunk? Agatha would have known."

"Why don't you call her?" Reiko said.

"Well, for one thing, I don't know her, and for another, I think she's dead. She was getting along in years."

"Gee," Reiko said, "if we could only call the police. My God! Why did you have to go around telling anybody and everybody??? Why???"

"Because I'm too honest. That's why!"

"Too dumb is better," Reiko said, and she was right. "Jesus," I said, "rat poison, a Colt .45, bear traps, a rope you can make a good noose out of. That's what I asked the guy in the hardware store!"

"He knew you were joking, didn't he?"

"Yeah, but he sold me the *rope!* He even showed me how to make a hangman's noose, like they used to do out West. This guy in the hardware store, he's a Clint Eastwood groupie."

Reiko couldn't believe this unlikely story. I couldn't myself, but that's the way it happened. My mother had told me when I was a little boy, "Keep your big mouth shut!" I never listened.

The telephone was ringing. I let it ring. I didn't want to talk to anybody. The telephone didn't stop ringing.

"Hello," I found myself saying. "What???? Who the hell are . . . ? Look, Mac, it's three o'clock in the morning! Who *is* this??? Lou Meskill? Oh, yeah. You're the feller who lives over on Thompson Street with the big dog that bites everybody. He's a *watch* dog? Jesus! He doesn't do much *watching*, but he sure does a helluva lot of *biting*. Now what was it you wanted at three o'clock A.M., Mr. Meskill? You and your wife have been having an argument? Interesting.

Yeah. About *what?* About that trunk that we bought at the auction? What about it? You want it *back?????*"

"My God!" I said to Reiko, who was almost past caring. "This clown wants his trunk back!"

"Tell him we sent it to Taiwan," Reiko said, which I really appreciated. I never would have thought of the perfect answer like that.

"Mr. Meskill," I said, "the trunk isn't here now. We sent it . . . we sent it to Taiwan. It's full of old clothes. I have this Taiwanese friend over there and he's got seventeen kids and they need . . . Oh, this is *Mrs.* Meskill. What? Your husband is on his way over here with a pickup truck . . . to pick up . . . your trunk—but, Mrs. Meskill!"

"She hung up," I told Reiko. "The trunk that they want back has sentimental value, it's been in the family since their honeymoon at Grossinger's."

Reiko couldn't believe this. "They took *that* trunk to Grossinger's on their honeymoon! My God! How *long* did they *stay?*" Then as an afterthought, "What do we do now?"

"I don't know about you," I said, "but I'm going to pieces!"

Reiko picked up the telephone, dialed quickly. "Hello, Old New Litchridge Police, this is Mrs. Jack Douglas up on Heigh-ho Road and . . . Yes, I *know* it's three o'clock in the morning. I'm sorry, but . . . Yes, next time I'll try to call earlier. Look, Sergeant, we have a complaint. Sergeant, I'm sorry, but I don't want to hear about your bad back and *your* complaints. Please, listen, there's a strange man in a pickup truck parked in our driveway and . . . No, I

don't know what color it is. He isn't here yet
. . . *Sergeant!*"

Reiko turned sadly to me. "He hung up."

"I wonder why?" It was all I could say. Just then we heard the roar of a pickup wheeling into our drive. Reiko quickly hurled a checkered tablecloth over the enormous trunk, slapped a vase of dead roses on top of that, along with two ashtrays, just as there was a pounding on our front door.

I opened it.

"Hi, I'm Lou Meskill. Sorry to bother you folks at this time of night, but the little woman insisted that I . . ."

"It's quite all right," I said. "Too bad you just missed your trunk. It's probably deep in the hold of the good ship, whatever, on its way to Hong Kong by now." (I looked at my wristwatch to check.)

"I thought you said 'Taiwan,'" Lou Meskill said.

"Stops at Hong Kong first," I said. "Right, Reiko?" Then I explained, "Reiko's Japanese, she knows all about ship movements in the Far East."

"Yeah," Reiko said, "Hong Kong, then Manila, Guam, Honolulu, Singapore, Bridgeport . . ."

"Huh?"

"We sent it United Parcel," Reiko said.

"United Parcel's on strike," Lou Meskill said.

"Aren't they always," I said. "Come on in. What are you drinking?"

"Beer will be just fine," Lou Meskill said.

"Beer?" I said. "Are you kidding? No beer in this house. Chivas Regal or nothing! [Then aside to Reiko.] Chivas Regal—a double."

103

Reiko was mighty quick to respond and Mr. Meskill was sitting there right in front of his disguised trunk with the largest double Chivas Regal that anybody anywhere had ever had before.

"Well, I dunno," Lou Meskill said.

"It's Arbor Day," I said. "Calls for a drink! You know, plant a tree, have a drink, plant a tree, have a drink. You'd be surprised how fast Arbor Day flies by!"

Suddenly Lou Meskill became aware of the "coffee table." "Jeez," he said, "that's the biggest coffee table I ever seen!"

"It *is* the biggest coffee table you've ever seen," Reiko said. "Formerly owned by a Ringling Brothers' circus giant—eight-foot-two, he was. He *needed* a big coffee table!"

Lou Meskill finished his huge double Chivas Regal in one gulp and held out his glass for a refill. Pretty good, I thought, for a guy who was hesitant about accepting anything stronger than beer.

Reiko refilled his glass with even greater alacrity than before. Lou Meskill gulped it down and we repeated the process. Finally he said, "You know, our honeymoon trunk used to be just about that size, spent a year at Grossinger's—swimming, ice skating, fishing, skiing, dancing, jogging, mountain climbing—and all indoors."

"How about eating?" I suggested.

"Oh my God!" Lou Meskill burped a good one even at this *mention*. "Six meals a day," he said. "Old Jennie Grossinger used to get sore as hell if you missed a meal or the midnight snack—roast duck and ap-

plesauce and seventeen different kinds of cheese-
cake."

"Yeah," I said, "well, it's getting late so why don't
you finish your drink and . . ."

Lou Meskill stood up—somehow. "Oh, I remember
you folks now. You're famous, it's all comin' back to
me. The Douglas's. Your baby nurse wouldn't leave
and you were gonna kill her. Yeah. How'd that come
out—she ever leave?"

Reiko and I looked at each other upon this unexpected burst of recognition and the question-and-
answer period.

"Well," I said, "—she's all packed."

"That's good," Lou Meskill said, leaning in a west-
erly direction, at about forty-five degrees. I didn't
know what was holding him up. "Those things usually
work themselves out."

"You can say that again," Reiko said.

"I'm afraid not, ma'am," Lou Meskill said. "You
see, I'm from Waterville, Maine, and we only say
things once."

I yawned a beautiful yawn, well calculated to hint
anybody into getting the hell out so we could go to
bed.

"I'm a little sleepy myself," Lou Meskill said.
"Here's the ten bucks you paid for the trunk."

"But," I protested, "we can't give it back to you because it's . . ."

"Look," he said, "I can't force you to give it back,
but . . ." He tapped the top of the checkered-table-
cloth-covered old trunk. "But if you only knew how
much this old trunk means to my wife." Lou Meskill

105

had suddenly taken charge. He removed the vase and the ashtrays and the checkered tablecloth and started to haul it toward the front door.

Lou Meskill did not get very far with the trunk. Suddenly he straightened up like he had ruined his back for life. "Oh, my God!" he said.

"Look, Mr. Meskill"—I thought I'd appeal to his baser instincts,—"I'll give you twenty bucks for that trunk."

"I'm sorry," Meskill said, "but, Jesus, I must be gettin' old, I can hardly budge this goddamned thing."

"Fifty bucks," I said.

Meskill kept trying to edge the trunk toward the door a half inch at a time.

"One hundred!" Reiko yelled, and the lights went on next door and Herb Hagedorn peered out the window to find out where the auction was going on.

"One hundred," Reiko repeated, coyly wiggling a little.

"Look," Meskill said, "you got the key to this thing? It seems to be loaded with something—something very heavy."

"It's our coin collection," I said. "We're sending it to Switzerland, you know, a Swiss bank so we won't have to pay any tax on it."

"That's dishonest."

"Of course it is—and I'm proud of my American ingenuity. And we don't have the key–I sent it to Saigon."

"I thought you said Taiwan before."

"Of course I did. But those Swiss banks gotta keep moving, they don't want anybody to know where the money is. So . . ."

106

"Well, I guess I'll just hafta have a key made. Ain't *nobody* gonna move this trunk, *loaded*. I'll make sure you get your coin collection back, Mr. Douglas."

"There's really no hurry, Mr. Meskill."

"We wanted to leave tomorrow, our second honeymoon."

"Oh?" *This* was *bad news!*

"Mount Rushmore is where we're headed." Meskill said.

"A second honeymoon at *Mount Rushmore!* Wow!" I said. "That's wild! Really *wild!*"

"Yeah, it's my wife's idea. She's kinda that way."

"Look," I said, getting desperate. I didn't know whether we were dealing with a nut here, or what. So far it hadn't sounded like we were conducting a seminar on anything pertaining to *this* world. "Mr. Meskill, why give yourself a hernia? I have this keymaker friend, John Charles Megenheimer, the Key Maker. You've seen his billboard out on the highway. I'll get him to make a key, we'll remove our coin collection and we'll send the trunk back to you, first thing in the morning."

"Yeah," Meskill said, "that sounds good and I'll only charge you twenty-five bucks."

"Twenty-five . . . bucks . . . *you'll* charge *us?*" Reiko was furious.

"You been *using* the *trunk*, haven't you?"

"Oh," I said, giving Meskill a real false chuckle. "I didn't look at it quite that way. Yeah." I chuckled again, this time even more phoney than the first time. "I'll see you in the morning, that'll be in about two hours." I ushered Mr. Meskill toward the front door, and just as he turned to leave I gave him a lovely kick right in his long overdue ass. Mr. Meskill stopped and turned around, slowly. Immediately I had second thoughts about my surreptitious attack.

Mr. Meskill took a deep breath while I held mine, then he said, positively and very quietly, *"Thirty-five bucks."*

"How about *forty*-five bucks and letting Reiko have a shot at you, too?" I said.

Meskill and I shook hands on this, and Reiko let go with a Kung Fu boot that sent him howling straight up in the air.

She *should* have waited until he turned around first.

CHAPTER

16

"WELL," I said, "Mr. Meskill has his trunk back and we have Mrs. Ogelvie back. Your idea of putting her in the deep freeze was *pure genius!*"

"Yeah," Reiko said, now up to smoking three cigarettes at one time, "but do you have any suggestions what the hell we are going to do with that rapidly melting one hundred pounds of chicken, two sides of beef, a year's supply of bacon, thirty pounds of ribs, fifty quarts of pistachio, orange walnut, and pecan-grape ice cream, twenty-five uncut kosher pastramis—all sitting in a lovely pile in the middle of the kitchen floor?"

"Well," I said, "maybe . . ." That's as far as I got.

"The water is two inches deep in there already," Reiko continued. "By six o'clock tomorrow morning, the washing machine and dryer, which are now on a collision course, will crash into each other and it will be the *Andrea Doria* all over again!"

"Don't fret yourself," I said, the picture of misplaced confidence.

"Don't fret myself!" Reiko was getting loud. "We'rc

in big trouble, as usual, and you try to make it sound like Sunday afternoon punting on the Thames!"

"Quiet a minute. Gimme time to think! I'll think of something!"

"Sure you will! In time, but the time is *now*! Every murder-mystery story I ever read, they're always hiding bodies in deep freezers, but they NEVER tell you what they do with all the stuff they take out of the freezer! What happens to it? We've got to *do something*—right—NOW!"

"I've got it!" I said. "A garage sale!"

"You're out of your mind!"

"I know, but what else is there! *What else*????"

"Maybe you're right," Reiko said. "Just maybe." Looking at her wristwatch, "It's only midnight. You get out in the garage, hang up a few Japanese lanterns, blow up a few balloons, and I'll start calling people." Reiko turned toward the phone.

"Wait a minute," I said. Reiko had given in too easily to my suggestion. "I have a better idea, why don't we just burn the garage down. We'll take Mrs. Ogelvie out of the freezer, first of course."

"Jack, the garage is attached to the house."

"Good," I said, "let the whole thing go! We'll start our lives anew—someplace else, change our name, start clean—just you and me and the baby. Oh my God! I just realized *something*! The baby, he's *never* been *baptized*!"

"What's that?"

"We take him down to the church, the minister sprinkles a little water on him and calls him whatever his name is and that's that."

110

"Why can't we take him to the temple?"

"He's not Jewish."

"The *Buddhist* Temple. All *they* do is bang the tom-toms for three hours, ring the bells, beat the gongs, sprinkle him with . . . with sweet and sour, I think it is—and call him whatever-his-name-is, Douglas."

"That's all there is to it?"

"Yeah."

"I got a better idea. There's a synagogue on the next block. Let's take him there. All they do is give him a beanie, say, 'Kid, you're Jewish, your name is *whatever* and get the hell out of here we got a pinochle game comin' up.' "

"Why are we *talking* at a time like this? I gotta get on the phone."

Reiko picked up the telephone and immediately there was a knock on the door.

Reiko froze.

I looked through the peephole in the front door. "It's Clyde, Mrs. Ogelvie's odd nephew."

"The one who saves mothballs?"

"Yeah, he puts 'em in separate little compartments in a fly-fishing case. He says if you keep 'em apart, they won't overbreed."

I opened the door to Clyde. He was a nice boy. Well-liked by everyone, except the people who had met him.

"Hello, folks," Clyde said, which no one can deny was a friendly enough greeting. "I just wanted to tell you . . . I was walking by and I just wanted to tell you, you left the light on in your garage."

"That's very nice of you to tell us about that, Clyde,

111

but we did it on purpose. We're cleaning up in there. You know how messy garages can become. Besides, we're having a garage sale."

"Oh, that sounds like good fun. When?" Clyde said.

"Tonight," Reiko said. "In fact, you are our first customer."

"Do I get anything for that?" Clyde immediately wanted to know.

"You get a hundred pounds of pastrami."

"Oh? Great!" Clyde was bubbling now.

"At cost," Reiko said.

Clyde bubbled off immediately.

"How would you like a year's supply of Canadian bacon?" I said.

"But I'm a Puerto Rican," Clyde said.

"No, you're not," I said. "You just *think* you are because you live in the South Bronx."

"Oh," Clyde said, relieved, I think.

"Maybe with Clyde here we won't have to tell anybody else about our garage sale," Reiko said.

"Now wait a minute," Clyde said (he was sharper than I knew), "I'm a bachelor and I don't do much cooking—TV dinners mostly. If you have any *Hungry Man* TV dinners, I'll take six. That'll keep me going for quite a while."

"Six, huh?" I said. "Well, I suppose we can break up a set and sell you just six, seeing that you're practically a relative, your Aunt Gladys—being somewhere around and all."

"If Auntie Gladys is up, I'd like to say hello to her," Clyde said.

"Oh, no," Reiko said quickly, "she hit the sack a long time ago."

112

"I hope she's okay," Clyde said. "She has this allergy."

"Oh, I don't think we have to worry about her allergy anymore," I said, quickly sitting on top of the deep freeze.

"What? Why?"

"Well, for one thing, she doesn't cough all over the place like she used to."

Reiko started to laugh but checked herself. I think she was once again on the verge of hysteria.

"What's so funny about not coughing?" Clyde asked.

"Mrs. Douglas is Japanese," I said. "The Japanese have a weird sense of humor, they think not coughing is funny. I saw an act in a nightclub in Tokyo—this comic came out on the stage and didn't cough for forty-five minutes and the audience thought he was hysterical! For an encore he came back and didn't cough for another twenty minutes! And just like *that* Ed Sullivan booked him for ten shows!"

"I'm gonna see if my Aunt Gladys is okay," Clyde said, then suddenly dashed upstairs to Mrs. Ogelvie's former room, now once again—ours. Clyde wasn't in there very long. He came downstairs again.

"Aunt Gladys isn't there. Her clothes are gone, too. Where did she go?"

"Cuba," I said. It was the only place I could illogically think of offhand.

"Cuba???? But why?"

"She's up in the hills there with a bunch of guerrillas. They're trying to overthrow Castro. Your Aunt Gladys felt she wasn't getting anywhere just being a plain baby nurse. She wanted a little adventure and

113

excitement, so she decided to become a mercenary in Cuba. She must be making at least a hundred bucks a day—as a mercenary."

"In Cuba?" Clyde was going into shock, so I had to continue.

"Yeah, that's something you didn't know about your Aunt Gladys. Your Aunt Gladys is a sharpshooter—been practicing on the sly for years."

"I didn't know she could shoot at all!"

"Clyde," I said, "you put your Aunt Gladys up in a palm tree with an M-16 and she can knock off a whole platoon in twenty minutes."

"What!!!!!"

"Maybe even more than that if they're Cubans. She's *great* on *Cubans!*"

Clyde fainted and Reiko threw a glass of cold Hawaiian Punch in his face to revive him. It didn't revive him, but it improved his complexion.

"What are you trying to do?" Reiko said.

"I'm just having fun," I said. "He doesn't know the difference."

"Where am I?" Clyde wanted to know, weakly.

"Don't worry, you're in good hands." I assured him.

"Mr. Douglas," Clyde laughed, "you're just having fun with me, aren't you?"

"Sure I am, Clyde," I said. "And don't you ever forget, I only have *fun* with *people I like*, and I like *you*, Clyde. You're a very nice boy. Your Aunt Gladys left us about ten o'clock this morning, I guess it was, or was it yesterday morning? Anyway, she's gone."

"Where?"

"To a better land we know," Reiko said.

114

"You're a big help," I said to Reiko.

"You make it sound like Auntie Gladys is dead," Clyde said.

"That's ridiculous," Reiko said.

I jumped in quickly. "Could *she* die? Ask yourself, Clyde. Could your Auntie Gladys die? *Ever??????*"

"Well, putting it that way, Mr. Douglas," Clyde said. "No! Not ever! She just *wouldn't go*!!!! Not while *Lawrence Welk is still alive*!!!"

CHAPTER

17

DESPITE the hour, the garage sale was more or less a success. I, because of my long, non-triumphant career as a stand-up nightclub comic, was the auctioneer.

"What am I offered for this full quart of (I had to read the label) pistachio-walnut-cherry-peppermint-chocolate-*tequila* ice cream?" I held up this container, which after its extended absence from its mother-freezer, was down to about a half a pint.

"Fifty cents," some sport in the back of the garage yelled.

"Sold," I said, "to the man in the pink pajama top."

The man in the pink pajama top, or maybe it was a shorty night shirt, came forward and gave me fifty cents in sticky pennies, then promptly drank down what was left in the container. "I didn't taste any walnut," he said and went back and sat down.

"What am I offered for this fifty-pound package of ribs?" I asked in my auctioneer's voice. There was no response at all.

"Anybody here from Harlem?" I asked.

A loud voice from the back of the garage. "It's three o'clock in the morning! Get to that side of beef!"

"Okay, okay," I said, wishing no trouble at my first auction. It might not be my last.

Reiko staggered out with a side of beef slung over her shoulder.

"Two dollars," the loud broad in the back belted.

"How would you like to go jogging in the Gowanus Canal?" I said suavely.

"Three dollars!" the voice again yelled.

"Look, Princess Margaret, this isn't a strawberry tart we're selling here, it's a side of beef—a one-hundred-pound side of beef!"

"Four dollars," came the screaming answer.

"Okay!!!!" I bellowed back. "Four dollars, Fat Mamma!"

A woman with a Bella Abzug hat came up, threw four old crinkly dollar bills on the table, picked up the side of beef like it was a chicken, and strode off into the night.

Reiko handed me the next item, which was a six-pound, frozen-solid leg of lamb. "What am I offered for this handy little weapon?" I asked, swinging it like a blackjack, with no thought of what I was doing.

"Hey, Jack!" Herb Hagedorn, our next-door neighbor, who was standing in the rear yelled, "Did you read that story in the *Reader's Digest* about the guy who killed his wife with the frozen leg of lamb and . . ."

CHAPTER

18

THE auction had been an ordeal, as well as non-profitable. Reiko and I were exhausted by the time the last neighbor had left with his or her half-thawed loot, but we still had work to do. The welder was coming at eight o'clock in the morning to weld the deep freeze shut so there wouldn't be any more close calls like we had at the auction. There were so many snoops who just wanted to take a peek in the box to see if we were holding anything out. They just walked into the kitchen, like it was their own, and started looking around. By chance we found out what was going on and locked up the whole area until the Great Event was over.

Unfortunately, we hadn't thought, ahead of time, of a very *good* reason *why* we wanted the deep freeze welded shut.

"If you'll pardon me for saying so, Mr. and Mrs. Douglas, this is a pretty nice brand-new deep freeze, and I have no objections to welding it shut for you, that's my job. But to bury your pet zebra in a brand-new deep freeze! Wouldn't it have been cheaper to just have somebody—*anybody* just build a cheap wooden box?"

"Yes," Reiko said, "but I just couldn't bear the thought of Rover being put in the cold, damp ground in nothing but a cheap wooden box." Reiko broke down completely and sobbed wildly.

"Gee," the welder said, "I didn't mean to—*Rover?*" A look of complete astonishment came over his face.

"Yes. I told you before," Reiko said. "That was our pet zebra's name. Oh, how quickly we forget." She sobbed again—but more discreetly this time.

"Gee," the welder said, again, "*I'd* never forget a zebra named 'Rover.' I don't think *anybody* would!"

"You'll have to forgive Mrs. Douglas if she's a little distraught," I told the welder. "I think it's the shock of having him go—so quickly."

"That's it," Reiko said, into her wet hanky. "One day he was here and the next day he was gone. He got hit by a car. I never should have let him off his leash."

"Yeah, well, I guess I better get started," the welder said. "This won't take very . . . " He stopped in midair, his torch blazing dangerously in all directions, "You were *walking* a *zebra* . . . on a leash?"

"Yes, every morning." Reiko broke down again. I didn't see how she could keep this up.

"Geez!" The welder was now talking to himself. "Gwen will never believe *this*—walking a zebra named Rover on a leash and it gets hit by a car. Gwen will never . . . "

"Gwen?"

"Oh," the welder said, "she's my wife. She *loves* animals."

"I'm glad to hear that," I said.

"Yeah, she's got a pet kangaroo, almost fifteen years old, getting a little deaf."

I thought we were getting the business from this welder, but if we were, you couldn't tell from his face. It was straight. He started to open the freezer and we both had a heart attack. We almost trampled him, stopping him from opening *anything*.

"No, no," I said, "we want to remember Trixie . . ."

"Rover!" Reiko yelled, digging me with her elbow.

"Yeah," I said, "Rover. We want to remember Rover as he was, big and full of life and—"

"I just wanted to check," the welder said. "Sometimes kids open these things, get inside, and nobody ever sees them again."

"Hi, what's up?" It was Clyde, Mrs. Ogelvie's nephew.

"Oh. Hello, Clyde, nice to see you again." I said.

Clyde quickly sized up what we were doing and said, "Say, if you don't want that deep freeze, I sure could use it. I gotta lotta cat food I gotta keep froze."

"You gotta lot of cat food?" Reiko said, drawing away from Clyde somewhat.

"Yeah."

"Why?"

"Gotta lotta cats. Almost fifty—or more. I didn't count since last Tuesday."

"I don't understand," I said. "Why would anybody have fifty or more—cats?"

"That's my *business*," Clyde said. "I'm an exterminator. *You* got rats, *I* got cats."

120

"Sounds very interesting." The welder stopped making sparks for just a moment to contribute.

"Yeah," Clyde agreed, "you got a house fulla rats. I just come with my cats, let 'em loose for fifteen or twenty minutes, and just like *that*—*no more rats*. Here's my card." He took out some cards, fanned them out like he was playing poker. "Go ahead," he said, swinging them around. We each took one (including the welder). The card read, "The Pied Piper Exterminating Co. *You* got *rats? We* got *cats!*"

"And," Clyde added, "if you don't pay me, I take out my magic flute and play it. Then I lead your kids away and you never see them again."

"Seems," the welder said, "you'd do more business with your *flute*. Forget about the cats."

"How about welding the deep freeze?" Reiko asked. "That's what we're all here for, isn't it?"

"You're *not* gonna give *me* the deep freeze, are you?" Clyde said.

"Sorry, Clyde," I said, "but a very sad thing happened. We're burying Spot, our pet zebra. He passed away in his sleep."

"Rover!" Reiko hissed. "And he was hit by a car."

Clyde was immediately concerned. "Rover? A zebra? What car? Whose?"

"Hit-and-run driver," Reiko said.

"The sonofabitch!" Clyde said.

"You can say *that* again," I said.

"No, I can't," Clyde said, "and that's the first time I *ever* said it!"

121

CHAPTER

19

AFTER the welder had gone back to his wife and her pet kangaroo with a hearing problem, and Clyde, disappointed that we had not been able to furnish him with the freezer for his cat food, also left us, we plugged it back in so Mrs. Ogelvie would keep fresh and cool. Our next problem was a momentous one: how did we get rid of an enormous 22-cubic-feet capacity freezer, now loaded with a two hundred-pound naked dead angel of mercy?

The first step was easy. I rented a Hertz U-Drive truck, a huge vehicle which I'm sure could have transported the Grand Coulee dam and Pearl Bailey at the same time. It was that sturdy.

Just backing this vehicle into our driveway took all day and most of our rose garden, carriage lamps, our lawn, and half of a hundred-year-old oak.

"Moving out, Jack?" Herb Hagedorn wanted to know.

"No," I said, and promptly turned and ducked into the house. I peeked through the kitchen window. Herb was still standing there, his mouth open. Then he called his wife and his three kids. They all stood there, looking at the Hertz behemoth with their mouths open. It looked like feeding time at a carp farm.

During the cocktail hour, the starting time of which we changed to suit ourselves (today it started before breakfast), Reiko and I tried to figure out how we would—if we *could*—transfer the extremely heavy deep freeze from the back porch to the flatbed of the enormous truck.

"Let's suppose," Reiko said, "let's just suppose we successfully get this deep freeze onto that big truck. Where are we going to drive it to get rid of the deep freeze and Mrs. Ogelvie?"

"That's a very good question," I said, and hoisted my third martini, successfully dumping it all over my frilly Mexican wedding shirt. It was very refreshing.

"I think," I said, "I can rig up a bunch of four-by-fours so we can hoist the deep freeze off the porch and onto the truck. Remember that block-and-tackle outfit we used to use in Canada to pull those great big pine trees off the house after the wind storms we kept having? Well, I kept that whole rig, in case someday we might need it. You always made fun of me for that, but you see, today—we *need* it!"

"Okay," Reiko said coolly, "so you were right—once."

"Now," I continued, after pouring another martini onto my ruffled Mexican wedding shirt, "after we get the body . . . I mean the freezer . . . loaded, where do we take it?"

"That's easy," Reiko said, pouring yet another martini onto my ruffled Mexican wedding shirt. "To the town dump!"

"The town dump!" I couldn't believe what I had heard. "That's the *first place* they'll *look!*"

"Who'll look?"

"Any scavenger who is looking for anything salvageable in the town dump. There are people picking over that dump *every* day—*nice* people. You'd be *surprised.*"

"What suggestions do *you* have?" Reiko asked snappishly.

"Well, I've done most everything during my lifetime except get rid of dead baby nurses, so I gotta think a little."

"Well??????" Reiko said, after a good five-second pause.

"Let's load the thing on the truck first," I suggested, without opposition.

It took two dark nights to get the deep freeze loaded onto the flatbed truck, with the aid of a very complicated derrick-like rigging which I concocted from pictures of the Straus-heel-type trunnion device used to raise and lower the bridges over the Chicago River. I have no idea of who Straus *was* or *is*, or what a heel-type-trunnion is, but it sure works with deep freezers loaded with dead bodies.

We had to turn the television set up real loud the second night to drown out the noise of the squealing rigging which, of course, was the wrong thing to do. We attracted a huge crowd of nosy neighborhood onlookers, which meant I had to *explain* what we were doing.

I started off, "A lot of you people probably wonder what we are doing here with all this equipment and this deep freeze. Well, I'll tell you what we are doing—we are proving once and for all that in *America,* *anyone* can do *anything* one *wants* to. And what *we* want to do is lift this deep freeze here—onto this big truck here!"

There were a lot of dissatisfied mumblings at this too logical explanation, but the crowd gradually dispersed and went back to their TV sets to watch the last fifteen minutes of the Three A.M. Matinee Movie, *Godzilla Tap Dances on Tokyo.*

Reiko and I left the loaded truck in the driveway and went back to the cocktail hour, still with no idea whatsoever where we were going to drop Mrs. Ogelvie.

"I'm gonna call my father," Reiko said and started to dial.

Reiko's father just happened to be in Japan, where he is a Buddhist priest, and it just happened to be four o'clock in the morning there—two days later, according to their time. But that didn't stop Reiko from calling. Buddha might have an idea.

After at least forty-five minutes of Japanese double-talk, Reiko hung up the telephone.

"What'd he say?"

"He wasn't there," Reiko said. "He was out looking for his dog. His dog is lost."

"Well, who the hell were you talking to for forty-five minutes, for Crissakes?!"

"His dog," Reiko said.

I grabbed Reiko by her long long long black black black hair. "What?"

"I'm just kidding," Reiko said. "I talked to my

mother, and my brothers and sisters, and just a little bit—to the dog."

I should have known because this had happened before. In Japan—on a long-distance call you had to talk to *everyone* in the family, including the dog, the parakeet, and the goldfish.

Reiko left word to have her father call later, collect, and after checking on the baby we went to bed.

Of course, the moment we got comfortable and cozy Reiko said, "I'm worried."

"I am, too," I admitted. "Pretty soon all those nosy neighbors out there are going to wonder what *really* happened to Mrs. Ogelvie. They're going to start to think about it. Then they're going to suspect us. The more they think, the more they'll suspect us of knocking off Mrs. Ogelvie, because—*where* is she? Would she leave without saying *goodbye* to *somebody?*"

"But we didn't knock her off! We didn't! We didn't! *We did not!!!!!*"

"As I said before, a hundred times, you think Walter Cronkite is gonna believe that?"

"What?"

"Or Mike Wallace???? *Particularly* Mike Wallace. Even when you haven't done *anything*, Mike Wallace *sends you to* the *chair!*"

The telephone rang. Insistently.

"Don't answer it," I said. Reiko said nothing, but she smoked three cigarettes in rapid succession. The phone was still carrying on. Reiko lit a fourth cigarette. I picked up the phone before Reiko found herself in need of resuscitation. It was the welder.

126

"Don't you know what time it is?" I asked.

"I didn't call to ask the time," the welder said. "I just wanted to know if you wanted me to stand by tomorrow. You know . . . "

"Stand by for what?"

"You know," the welder said, "in case you change your mind and wanted your deep freeze unwelded *open* so you can take a last look at your dear departed. I can give you a rate. You know—two welds for the price of one." I said nothing. There was quite a pause.

"Am I interrupting?" the welder asked. "You got company?"

"Jesus! Joseph! And Mary!" I yelled.

"Oh?" the welder said. "They back together?"

"God'll getcha for that!" I said.

"Call you first thing in the morning," the welder said and hung up.

Reiko lit a whole pack of cigarettes at once, and I opened a secret compartment in my back bar and took out a case of Gilbey's and proceeded to make a vaseful of martinis, without the gentling caress of vermouth and sans the lullaby of tinkling ice. Then I sat down, very carefully, on my rhino-horn easy chair. Actually, there is nothing easy about a rhino-horn easy chair, cleverly constructed of thirty-two screwed-together rhino horns. A miscalculation of an inch or two in sitting down and you could very easily give yourself what is known to former big-game hunters as a Serengeti high colonic.

"Who was that?" Reiko wanted to know. I didn't answer. I was too busy reassuring myself that gin makes you drunk about as quickly as anything else alcoholic.

127

"Who was that?" Reiko, again, wanted to know, somewhere within a fogbank of cigarette smoke. "The police?"

"Why would the police call us," I said, "especially at three o'clock in the A.M.?"

"Why not? We're murder suspects, aren't we?"

"Well, I wouldn't . . . I started to hedge."

"Well, *I* would," Reiko said.

I knew she was right. What else could the police or anyone, outside of Billy the Kid, think? I had been loudmouthing it all over town about how I would like to knock off Mrs. Ogelvie. I had bought rat poison, ant poison, gopher poison, boll weevil poison, and borrowed a Colt .45 from the druggist. Circumstantial evidence, you say?—Yeah.

I had even gone so far as to call the employment agency and tell them if Mrs. Ogelvie spent one more night with us she'd never see tomorrow morning. And, just to make sure of putting my head in the noose, the whole thing had been recorded on tape (*their* tape), right after the recorded voice said, "When you hear the tone leave your message."

I left my *message*! Like bloodied fingerprints!

"Well" —I started to make a second vase of martinis and console myself—"*cherchez la femme*," I said. Then I repeated it, "*Cherchez la femme*."

" What the hell does that mean?" Reiko said.

"It's French. It means either 'Find the woman' or 'Please do not spit against the wind.' Are you trying to *smoke* us to *death*?" I said, as as wall of silver-blue carbon monoxide and mustard gas rolled toward me from somewhere where Reiko was coughing like a

128

bass Camille. She sounded like she was at the bottom of a deep well.

"For Godsakes! Don't you see the sign *Be It Ever So Humble—No Smoking!*" I said, lying with my face close to the floor like the Fire Department tells you to do.

"That's the way it goes," Reiko said, "as soon as the honeymoon is over. My father warned me."

"Your father warned you not to marry an American, that's all. He didn't mention anything else. Would you rather be married to a Buddhist priest like your father wanted? With all those gongs and tom-toms bang bang banging?"

"*You* promised me *silver bells,*" the voice in the smoke said—wistfully.

"Balls!" I said.

"Silver *balls?*" Reiko said.

"Look, let's not sit here misunderstanding each other tonight. We've been doing that for two years. Let's sit here and figure out what we are going to tell the druggist, half the town, and last but not least, the police. They'll be here any minute."

Reiko emerged from the smoke and floated across the room to me and my martini vase. "Why should the police be here any minute?" I finished my vase and started to make another before I answered.

"Because I imagine Clyde probably went to them and complained that his Aunt Gladys is missing."

"I don't think so." Reiko shook her head, trying to smile.

"Look," I said, "that kid is a dope, but he's no dope."

"Hold it," Reiko said, raising her hand like she was

129

commanding the Red Sea to stop fooling around and open up—as promised.

"That kid is a dope, but he's no dope?" she said.

"Well," I said, sitting down, not carefully, and rising so quickly as to hit my head on the cross-eyed moose we have hanging way up on our fieldstone fireplace. Everywhere you go in our house—*horns.*

"I've been gored!" I said. "Where are the wills?"

"Huh?"

"The wills! I want to check 'em—make sure *you're* named!"

Reiko pursed her lips, "That's the way you've always been," she said, "everything at the last minute!"

"Look," I said, "of course it's the last minute. You don't make out a will the moment you spring from your mother's womb. Unless, of course, you're very rich and to spite some showgirl in Las Vegas, you want to leave everything to your wife."

"I don't know what that means," Reiko said, "but I think I'll go back to Japan. NOW!"

"*Oh, no,*" I said, "you *can't,* and even if you do, they got Interpol—they'll bring you back here. *You* gotta face a *murder rap,* baby."

"Bullshit!" Reiko said (in Japanese). In Japanese it's the only word I *really* understand—*perfectly.*

CHAPTER

20

THREE days late we still had the U-Drive truck sitting in our drive with the deep freeze sitting in the middle of its flatbed.

My next-door neighbor, Herb Hagedorn, waited as long as I guess he thought he should, then he stuck his bald head through the hedge which separated our vast fifty-foot lots in Old New Litchridge Estates and said, "I don't want to seem to be butting in, Jack, old chap, but what is that?" nodding in the direction of the U-Drive and its cargo. "Some sort of a monument or something?"

By this time, the same graffiti artists who had decorated the Sherman tank in the village green had done the same job on our deep freeze. Same job and same theme. Four-letter suggestions in every language from Old English to young Yiddish.

"Yes, Herb, it *is* a monument. You remember Mrs. Ogelvie?"

"Your kid's nurse that you were gonna kill?"

"That's the one," I said. "It's a monument to her."

Herb Hagedorn seemed puzzled for a moment, then he said, still puzzled, "You mean like a *memorial* monument?"

"You got it." I said. "You got it the first time."

"You mean she's gone?"

"She's gone."

"She's not coming back?"

"She's not coming back."

"You *didn't?*"

"I said I was *going* to, didn't I?" I said. "You know anybody *you* want knocked off?" I said. "Like maybe your boss, or some lawyer—lawyers I do cheap. I can give you a rate if you want the whole firm taken care of . . . "

Herb Hagedorn started backing off a little, I thought. His unhaired head was disappearing into the shrubbery like a harvest moon behind a field of ripe marijuana. It became apparent that Herb had discovered that he had been exchanging small talk with an overly eager psychopath.

For a moment I got sentimental and toyed with the idea of spray-painting some memorial-type words of my own on Mrs. Ogelvie's Birdseye tomb. Maybe something like *She Now Belongs To The Ages* or *Win A Trip To South Bend—Guess How Many Jellybeans in This Box?*

"What are we gonna do with that deep freeze?" I asked of no one in particular during a commercial break while I was watching the Carson show, or maybe it was Griffin, or Mike Douglas, or maybe it was a local show, known to the local audience as the crookedest show on the air. It was called *Bowling For Bucks,* and the reason we all knew it was crooked was because on *Bowling For Bucks* they used square balls and the pins were screwed into the floor.

Nobody ever won, but they had a consolation prize for the losers—a free game.

"What deep freeze?" Reiko said, vaguely because she wasn't paying any attention to the outside world. She was into what seemed to be becoming her life's work—wallpapering our living room with scenes from *War and Peace* (a new direction in the trendy sphere of interior decorating)—scenes from history or famous novels, and if your living room was large enough you could reproduce *War and Peace* from beginning to end, or if you just had a small studio apartment you could have *one* scene from *Lady Chatterly's Lover. Which* scene, of course, would depend on your neighborhood. Or your wife. Or your roommate. Or both.

"Look," I said, "this is very important. What are we going to do with that deep freeze? It's brand-new. And I gotta get that U-Drive truck back. It's costing us fifty-four dollars a day—and gas."

"Oh," Reiko said, dropping the gooey brush back into the paste bucket and wiping her hands on her very untidy apron, "fifty-four dollars a day! Maybe we should take a trip somewhere."

"Yeah," I agreed, "maybe Mexico! It's only about two thousand miles from here, and maybe we can hide out in the hills and become peons or peasants or something. We can bury the truck in the sand."

"How would we get home?" Reiko asked.

"We're not coming home," I said. "You know what it's like to sit in a six-by-eight-foot prison cell for the rest of your life?"

"But *we didn't*—!"

"I *know!* I *know!* We've been *through* all that!"

133

"But . . ."

"I think I'll ask Clyde to help me get the deep freeze down off the truck and back into the house. People are starting to talk. We've left it out in the driveway too long."

"Look," Reiko said, "I don't want that thing back in the house, even after we get rid of Mrs. Ogelvie. I have no intention of ever using it again, not after she's been *resting in peace* in there all this time."

"She's not '*resting in peace!*' She's *dead, very dead. Not resting!* That's the same kinda sweet talk your friendly neighborhood undertaker gives you when he wants you to buy a more *expensive box*—one with a *silk lining* and a velvet cushion for the *Loved One's* head. They don't tell you that the *Loved One* isn't wearing anything below his waist, and his lonely butt is *resting in peace* on a *splintery hunk of number-three-grade plywood!* Also the *Loved One's* gold teeth have been removed, and any rings that have been nostalgically left on the *Loved One's* fingers were filed off the first day the *Loved One* rested in peace in a 32-degree seven-foot *filing cabinet!*"

"You know something, Jack," Reiko said.

"What?"

"You make *Forest Lawn* sound like it's *no fun at all!*"

CHAPTER

21

"LET'S go to bed," Reiko said. It wasn't an invitation. It was a weary suggestion.

We had been sitting in our once cozy living room, staring at our empty fireplace and its lonely andirons, which in happier times had held a jolly pile of gas-fired simulated yule logs but now held nothing. Not even hope. And certainly no promise of Christmas joy to come. Our precious antique Grandfather clock, which stood in the hall, struck nine times, so we knew it was at least twelve midnight. Or maybe one A.M. Or it could be eleven P.M. Or then again—three o'clock the next afternoon.

We had been sitting for hours, speaking only intermittently about our problem and solving nothing.

Mrs. Ogelvie was still outside in her General Electric sepulcher on the U-Drive truck.

"I remember a movie," Reiko said. "These two guys—I think it was Richard Widmark and Vincent Price—they take this body they want to get rid of and they put it in a car. Then they drive it to one of those car-crushing places. You know, it's like a garbage compactor. They drive it into this bin. It's a Volkswagen and the machine crushes it into the size of a breadbox."

"What about the body?" I wanted to know.

"Oh—it's there in the breadbox—somewhere—Who knows?"

"That's not a bad idea," I agreed, "but with Mrs. Ogelvie, a Volkswagen wouldn't do. We'd have to use a Cadillac Eldorado or—a school bus."

Again, our old Grandfather clock wound up and got ready to strike the hour, but somehow there was no sound at all. Just a sigh.

"It's getting late," I said, not without some calculation.

"Who do we know with a car-crushing machine?" Reiko asked.

"They don't rent things like that and we don't know a soul with a car-crushing machine, and it serves us right."

"What's that mean?" Reiko said, bristling.

"It means," I said, "when we moved here to Old New Litchridge we should have *mixed* a little like I suggested. By this time we'd know *all* the car-crushing-machine owners for miles around."

"If we knew somebody who owns an elephant."

"What?"

"An *elephant!* You know, a big gray thing with long white things curving out in front and big feet. It could stamp a school bus flat in no time."

"How about an octopus? It could *tear* it apart eight ways."

We were getting silly.

136

"I think I heard something," Reiko said. "Don't turn on the lights."

"You heard something? Where?"

"Outside. Maybe somebody is fooling around with the deep freeze, trying to steal something!"

"It's welded shut!"

"*We* know that—but *they* don't!"

"Who don't?"

"Look out the window! Somebody backed another flatbed truck up to our flatbed truck and they got a deep freeze just like ours."

"What the hell are they trying to do?"

"Oh," Reiko said, giggling, almost in hysteria, "isn't that super! They are exchanging *their* deep freeze for *our* deep freeze."

"They must be nuts!"

"No, ours is brand-new and theirs looks like an old one. It doesn't have that little orange light on the side like ours does."

"Jeez! They're really prepared. There's four of them!"

"Yeah—and they're not kids either."

And they weren't. There were two older men and two younger women, maybe in their thirties. I could see quite plainly in the bright moonlight.

"I don't understand," Reiko said. "Why don't they just steal our deep freeze and go? Why leave a replacement?"

"They don't want us to find out. Supposing we should go out there right after they leave and see that our deep freeze is gone. We'd call the cops. I mean— *theoretically* we'd call the cops. This way it might be *days* before we discovered they'd stolen our brand-new deep freeze."

"They must have been casing this job for quite a while," Reiko said.

"*Casing this job*," I said. "Where'd you get that kinda talk?"

"When we lived in New York. Everybody on the subway used to talk like that."

There was a loud crash outside.

"Holy Buddha! They dropped our deep freeze!"

"Don't worry. It's welded shut!"

The lights came on all over the house next door.

A window slammed open.

"Hey, what's going on out there?????" It was Herb Hagedorn. He didn't miss a thing in our neighborhood. Or in the whole town.

"We just dropped a deep freeze," one of the four deep-freeze thieves responded, normally and naturally.

"Oh," Herb said, "—need any help? I'd be glad to . . . "

"No," said the voice, "we'll manage quite nicely, thank you."

"Okay," Herb said, then as a brilliant afterthought, "Have a good weekend."

"Thank you," the voice answered. Herb closed his window and switched off all his lights.

"They act like *we* weren't even *home*," Reiko said.

"Our lights aren't on and it *is* a weekend. They figure we're away," I said.

During the next few moments the four thieves were very active and *our* deep freeze was on *their* flatbed and *theirs* was on *ours*. They drove out the driveway like it was the start of the Indianapolis 500 and were gone.

"Thank you, dear God," I said. "Mrs. Ogelvie now belongs to the ages."

"I wouldn't be too sure," Reiko said. "What do you suppose they'll do when they find out she's inside? They'll go running to the cops and tell them everything!"

"Tell them *everything*?????!!!!!" I was *shouting*! Herb Hagedorn's window opened and shut.

I started to whisper. "Tell the cops that they were stealing a deep freeze from our driveway, and when they got it wherever, they found a dead body in it? These guys are *professional thieves*, they aren't going to tell *anybody anything*. Let's go out and see what kind of deep freeze they left. We probably can use it."

CHAPTER

22

THE deep freeze the crooks left looked just about like the one they stole from us. I plugged it into our outdoor socket and it worked.

"We're in luck," I said. "We got a hot deep freeze that works."

"What do you mean a 'hot' deep freeze?" Reiko asked.

"Stolen. That's what we say in America when something is stolen. We call it hot."

Reiko opened the lid and immediately shrieked. Herb Hagedorn's window shot up.

"What is it?" he yelled.

"None of your goddamn business!" I yelled back, as I caught a glimpse of the inside of our new deep freeze. There was a naked body in there—a man's body. What we had here, I thought, was the victim of a gangland rub-out.

"Jesus!" Herb said. "Why didn't I move into a *black* neighborhood? When *they* get loaded, they don't *yell*, *they sing!*" Then, to us, "Honky *bastards!*" The window slammed down.

"Get Mr. What's-his-name, the welder, on the phone," I commanded Reiko.

"Now?" she said.

"Now!" I said. "Right *NOW!*"

It was almost dawn when the welder left, well satisfied with his quadruple pay for overtime. Reiko and I dropped into bed like two bags of wet cement.

The old Grandfather clock in the hall banged out fifteen bong-bongs and the alarm clock started to clang like the house was *on fire.* After I looked out the window at the flatbed truck, I wished that it were. The truck was right where it had always been, but next to our last-night-acquired deep freeze stood our *old brand-new* deep freeze! It had been *returned!* I was stunned. We now had two deep freezers more than we ever needed, and we were sure that Mrs. Ogelvie was back (although she hadn't known that she had been away).

We checked her freezer, and there she was—smiling up at us through her fat. I slammed the freezer lid shut just as Herb Hagedorn's window flew open.

"There gonna be a shortage?" Herb wanted to know.

"Shortage of what?" I said.

"Deep freezers?" Herb said, reasonably enough.

"Oh," Reiko said, "it's not that. It's just that our almost-new baby loves ice cream and we just can't seem to keep enough of it in the house and . . . "

"*I* never saw a baby," Herb said.

"Neither did we for quite a while there, but we see him all the time now."

"He's cute," I said. "Got red hair, just like his mother."

141

"Reiko's hair is black," Herb said, quick as a wink.

"It has to be black," Reiko said. "I'm Japanese."

"You're *kidding!*" Herb said. Herb had quite a sense of humor, especially early in the morning before breakfast. "Well," he said, "gotta get down to the bank."

"This is Sunday," I said. "You're a vice-president of the bank. You gotta work on *Sundays?*"

"Not really," Herb said, "but when you're a vice-president and *also* an *embezzler,* it keeps you pretty busy." Herb closed his window quickly.

"Someday I'm going to kill him," I confided to Reiko.

"Good," Reiko said. "What we need is another dead body."

"Yeah," I agreed, "and maybe we can arrange to get our deep freezers wholesale. They must be cheaper by the dozen. Do we know twelve people we don't like in Old New Litchridge?"

"Better order *two* dozen," Reiko suggested.

CHAPTER

23

MRS. OGELVIE'S Birdseye box had been unwelded by the recent crooks, so we had to have Virgil and his torch back again.

"How about me reporting in every morning about eight," he said, "just in case you need me."

"I don't think so," I said, "but it's very considerate of you to suggest it."

"Yeah," Virgil said, "and at thirty bucks a visit I'm makin' almost as much as a cheap doctor."

"Goodbye, Virgil," Reiko suggested and he left.

"Jack, we're all out of eggs. I've got to go to the store. We've been out of eggs for ten days now."

"So?"

"So move the truck, I've got to get the car out."

"*Move the truck!!!!!*" I threw myself on the floor and started kicking my heels in probably the best tantrum I had ever thrown—but I moved the truck.

I got it out into the street and into a two-hour parking zone.

"Thank you, dear," Reiko said. "I won't be long. Then you can move the truck back into the driveway."

"I'm leaving the keys in the truck," I said, "and I'm

also putting little signs on both sides of the hood. 'Isabel, the keys for the truck are on top of the sunshade.'"

"Who's Isabel?" Reiko wanted to know.

"Oh my God! How the hell do I know?" I screamed. "That's just a name I put on the sign so somebody'll see the sign and maybe steal the truck and our troubles will be over."

"Just our luck somebody will steal the truck, then bring it back with *three* deep freezers on it."

"That's ridiculous," I said. "Where they gonna get another body?"

"Don't you read the papers?" Reiko said. "There are thousands of nuts running around with guns, knives, baseball bats, blackjacks, rifles, telephone cords, pantyhose . . . "

"What?"

"Pantyhose, that's the new thing they're using. You know—the Boston Strangler, the Hartford Strangler, the Burbank Strangler—those guys."

"Funny we don't have a strangler in Old New Litchridge," I said. "It's so *right!*"

"It's still a small town," Reiko said.

"We have the Old New Litchridge Flasher," I said.

"Yeah, and he's got a brand-new day-glo raincoat—I saw him yesterday standing out in front of the library. He flashed at everybody that came out of the library—and nobody paid any attention to him."

"That's because he's an amateur. He just doesn't know how to flash! Somebody should tell him a genuine flasher does *not* wear long winter underwear and a crotch corsage—it kills the whole concept!"

144

"Well, I've got to go before the baby wakes up and wants something."

"For heaven's sake, don't buy anything we have to keep very long," I said.

"Oh," Reiko said, "I was planning to pick up a couple-a dozen frozen pizzas."

"Okay," I said. "We'll put them in with the gangster."

"Is he Italian?" Reiko asked.

"What difference does it make?" I said. "He's dead—how many can he eat?"

Reiko didn't even smile. She just slipped into her shoplifting coat and left for the A & P.

CHAPTER

24

AFTER Reiko got back with a load of eggs, I put two dimes in the on-street parking meter, just in case we were being watched, and backed the U-Drive truck up the driveway and dumped a lot of grass clippings on the hood. This was in the hope that this monster-vehicle would look to the untrained eye like part of our meticulous landscaping. It would have to be a mighty untrained eye, but I was desperate.

"Is everything all right?" Reiko asked.

"Why not?"

"I just thought that one of the freezers moved a little when you drove into the driveway."

What the hell, I thought! Reiko is going bananas with all this stress. And why not? How did she know when we got married that we'd have to spend our happy life together hiding corpses!

"Which freezer moved?" I had to go along.

"The one with Mrs. Ogelvie in it."

"My God! Maybe she's still alive! How could that be? No," I convinced myself with difficulty, "it's your imagination—or maybe you're crazy," I added, diplomatically. Nevertheless, I thought Reiko's hallucinations warranted investigation. I moved out into the area in back of the house and crouched my way up to

146

the huge U-Drive. Everything was fine. Both freezers were welded shut and neither was levitating.

"Hey!" A voice from nowhere scared me shitless, to put it delicately.

"Hey. Over here!" It was my next-door-and-everywhere-else neighbor Herb Hagedorn. "You see my golf ball?" Herb wanted to know. "You can't miss it, it's painted red, white, and blue and it has my name on it in *neon*."

"How could you *lose* it?" I was snotty.

"Well, I might as well confess," Herb said. "I'm sorta nearsighted and sometimes even the neon doesn't help much, except, of course, at night."

"Who the hell plays golf at night?" I was getting snottier.

"*I* do," Herb said. "They keep me so late at the bank. I'm the *loan officer*, you know, *we* have the *mortgage* on *your* place, you know."

"How would you and your mortgage like to take a flying fuck for yourselves?" I asked him, not snotty this time. Sweet like Crazy Joe Gallo.

"A *flying* fuck?" Herb mulled this. "Sounds like *fun*. I saw some pictures once in an old *National Geographic*. Did you know that Genghis Khan used to do it on horseback—upside down?"

"What?"

"It's true," Herb said. "He didn't have any bedrooms at all at the palace, just stables, a riding ring—and a ringmaster with a long whip. Poor Genghis! He had to give it up after a while."

"Why?"

"It gave the horses a headache."

I had to ask.

CHAPTER

25

"YOU know," Reiko said, "there's a place near here called *Lovers' Leap.*"

"Hooray," I said.

"Banzai!" Reiko said.

"Is that all there is to your travelogue?" Reiko was a little angel, but I was in no mood to categorize.

"Lovers' Leap is where lovers go to leap," Reiko said.

"Thank God you explained," I said. "I would have spent the rest of my life trying to figure out why Lovers' Leap was called Lovers' Leap instead of Broadway and Forty-second Street. And I told you about Lovers' Leap a long time ago."

"There's a deep gorge there—" Reiko was being tolerant "—a very deep gorge, and there's a bridge—and every once in a while some drunk drives his car off the bridge and down down down into the gorge."

"Three *downs!* It must be pretty deep."

"It is. Almost a thousand feet. And there's a river at the bottom—a *deep deep deep* river!"

"Three *deeps*, must be . . . "

"Pretty deep," Reiko concluded for me. "It's not

only deep, but the river is very fast at that point, very fast."

"*Fast fast fast?*" I asked.

"I wasn't going to say that."

"Are you suggesting we take the truck and the two freezers and drive the whole thing off the Lovers' Leap Bridge?"

"If *drunks* can do it, *we* can do it," Reiko said, with the inscrutable logic of the Oriental.

We had Virgil, the welder, back again. If he was surprised he didn't say anything. Maybe because he knew he had a good thing going with us. After he un-welded both the freezers, and we made sure he didn't peek, we took him inside and gave him a good shot of our cheapest whiskey.

"See you later," Virgil called as he drove off in his Silver Cloud.

I hoped that that had not been a prophecy. We should soon know.

We decided not to use the U-Drive truck for the Lovers' Leap affair because it would entail more ex-planation than we were prepared for, and we wanted the extreme Status Quo in regard to our situation. We wanted to leave the U-Drive truck and the two freez-ers in our driveway just as they were now and would be when the accident at Lovers' Leap was discovered.

That is why we chose to make use of Herb Hage-dorn's handy brand-new Buick station wagon. It was handy because it was always parked in the driveway next door and also because Herb never removed the

149

keys, no matter how long and loud the *"you-left-your-keys"* buzzer buzzed its warning of the dire consequences of such carelessness.

Never having been a car thief before, I slipped into a pair of shiny black gloves and had three double martinis (I knew from reading Raymond Chandler that fingerprints should *never* be left on *double martinis*, especially if you are planning to make off with your neighbor's station wagon at the stroke of midnight).

While Reiko watched Herb Hagedorn's bedroom window with binoculars, I sweated considerable blood as I quietly backed his car down his driveway and out toward the deathly quiet, deserted street. Inch by inch, I eased it down the slope and onto the pot-holed surface of Heigh-ho Road.

I breathed a long, *premature* sigh of relief because almost immediately it *happened!* A sound like the twenty-minute air battle in *The War of the Worlds* compressed into one mighty three-second smash!

I had bumped something! And it was only then that I noticed that Herb Hagedorn's brand-new station wagon was hitched onto a brand-new super-camper! It was at least forty feet long, with three canoes in launching racks on top—enormous rubber bumpers like the ones that are used on tugboats lining the sides, and a gigantic stainless-chrome steel protective battering ram, welded, riveted, and bolted onto its rear. A super-camper with an awesome behind like that would *never* be tailgated!

How I missed seeing this monster hitched to the wagon I'll never never know. Maybe I had had *four* doubles. With martinis who can count?

150

I was out of the car like a snake and back in the house with Reiko.

"What was that?" Reiko asked.

"What was what?" I said, keeping my eyes laser-beamed right at Herb Hagedorn's bedroom window.

"I thought I heard something," Reiko said.

"You did," I said, still staring at the little house on the prairie next door, but nothing happened. No flinging up of windows, no flood lights, no screams of panic. Not from Herb's house. Not from anywhere in the whole area.

"I think," I said, "I think everybody is dead."

Reiko shook her head sadly. "Well," she said, "there goes the neighborhood."

At the scene of the impact, everything was much worse than I had anticipated. I had backed Herb's super-camper across the street and up the across-the-street driveway of another neighbor, Cle Mahoney, a boat nut. And what I had done was gun the rear of Herb Hagedorn's battering-ram super-camper into the stern of Cle's newest aquatic acquisition, a forty-seven-foot deep-sea cruiser with a thousand-mile range, a flying bridge, and two five-hundred-gallon fuel tanks filled to their gills with number-three diesel oil. This was a condition destined not to prevail. Not with Herb's probing super-camper-back-end deep within their bulging bowels. Within seconds the gutters of Heigh-ho Road were twin Tennyson's Brooks—oiling their ways down to the sea.

Reiko made a suggestion which I thought was a good one. "Let's get this over with quick!" she hissed.

That did it for me. In an instant I was back in Herb's car, standing on the gas pedal, tearing Herb's super-camper out of Cle's cruiser with a horrendous rip! I pulled over to the curb and waited for the wrath of all of Old New Litchridge to descend on us. But nothing. It was the mystery of the ages. They couldn't all have gone away for the weekend. Or maybe they had left for good and hadn't told us about the latest thing in viruses—the *Swahili* flu. Not a window opened. Not a light was turned on. Not even in a bathroom.

"Hurry," Reiko said, "unhitch that goddamn camper!"

Another superior suggestion, and I tried everything but dynamite and a couple of more martinis, but Herb's station wagon and Herb's super-camper were as one. They were not to be parted. Not in this lifetime.

"What are we gonna do?" Reiko said.

"Nothing," I said. "Herb's station wagon and Herb's super-camper and our Mrs. Ogelvie and our little hoodlum are *all* going to go off the Lovers' Leap Bridge *together*. We can't break up a set!"

Getting Mrs. Ogelvie's frozen-stiff body out of the deep freeze was like trying to transplant the redwoods. She was solid ice and slippery, and immediately after we got her in the back seat of Herb's station wagon she slipped down to the floor among the hundreds of McDonald Big Mac cartons that Herb seemed to be hoarding.

The gangster was a cinch. He was lighter and he had died with an erection so he was easier to handle. We put him in the front seat between us, because

152

when he and Mrs. Ogelvie went off Lovers' Leap together—*he* would be driving.

We passed Jim Harkness in a police car on the way to our rendezvous with destiny. He waved and we waved back. We had no way of knowing whether he thought he was waving to Herb or Reiko and me, but we didn't have much time to think about that.

We crossed the Lovers' Leap Bridge twice before we picked a spot where the railings looked less firm and the river would be the deepest. It was a fairly wide bridge and I drove over to the left side of it and pointed the front wheels to the right side of it, roughly in the direction of Danbury. I slid the gangster over behind the wheel, put the car in second gear, held down the brake, and was just about to wire the gas pedal when a car came roaring up the hill and onto the bridge. He must have been going at least seventy and he kept right on coming, straight for *Herb Hagedorn's car!* I switched the lights on and off in warning and at the last possible moment he careened around us, screaming something about "Bastards!" But he kept right on going, which made us bastards get down on our knees and thank the angel that watches over bastards. I wired the gas pedal down and let her go.

Herb's car shot across the bridge like it had been fired from a cannon. It slammed into the guard rail and stopped—*dead!* The guard rail was tougher than I thought. How did the drunks get through it, I wondered? Maybe they had reinforced it since the last drunk.

153

"Try again," Reiko yelled, "before anyone else comes along!"

I tried again. This time from right to left. I put it in first gear this time and tied the gas pedal *way* down. It now had *twice* the power. Across the bridge roadbed it *leaped* and *crunch*! It was stopped cold by the opposite guard rail.

I tried three more times, each time with the same result. By now Herb's car was a crumpled mass of mess. Mrs. Ogelvie had disappeared from sight under the mountain of McDonald's Big Mac containers and the gangster was upside down, his face on the floor and his erection, which hadn't quelled one bit, held his rear end up and over the back of the seat.

Then the same car which had almost rammed us before was back. This time it stopped.

"Need any help, folks?" a voice said.

"No thanks," I said, almost stuttering. "We can manage."

"Just thought I'd ask," The voice said. "I belong to the Big Brothers. We always like to help."

"Yeah. Well, thanks," I said. "It's very nice of you. I'm an Elk."

"What the fuck do *they* know!" came another voice from the car. "Come on, Merv, we gotta get back to the 'Y.'" And the car left, very suddenly.

"Well," I said, "we've still got a few more hours till daylight. Let's give it another try."

"Better check the camper first," Reiko said.

"Why?" I wanted to know. "We can't get it loose. We tried, remember?"

"No," Reiko said, "I didn't mean *that*. Every time you hit that guard rail with Herb's car, Herb's camper

154

swings around like you're playing snap the whip and whacks into the rail. The whole back end looks like a ten-foot can of Budweiser that was squeezed by the Jolly Green Giant."

I checked the camper through its picture windows; the driver's seat, the breakfast nook, the sleeping quarters, the living room, the dining room, the library, the shower room, the sauna, and the toilet were now as *one*. Everything was neatly crushed into a huge ball, colored here and there and everywhere by bright splashes of book covers, Delft china, paper napkins, Oriental rugs, chintz curtains, and what looked like a year's supply of spaghetti sauce (Herb was a hoarder). The seat of the toilet was hanging open and swinging (it was gasping for air).

"Everything seems to be all right," I assured Reiko, and took a long drag on a bottle of 180 proof vodka I had had the good sense to bring along.

Reiko looked at me as though I had suddenly lost my senses, which wasn't too unusual.

"All right?" she said. "Look at that beautiful camper! It looks like it's been whipped by one of those big iron balls they use to slap down buildings!"

"Hello, folks—camping?"

Reiko and I jumped into each other's arms. Who the hell?????

It was a little old lady wearing alpine boots and carrying an eighty-pound pack that loomed overhead like the tilting rock. In her right hand she carried a shepherd's crook and in her left a large flashlight.

I *had* to ask her, "Lost your sheep?"

"Oh—this?" she said. "No—this just helps me to walk. I'm a veteran."

I didn't ask her of *what?*

"What about the flashlight?" Reiko said.

"It's night," the little old lady reasonably explained.

"And it's raining," Reiko said.

"Mind if I knock off forty winks in your camper?" the little old lady asked. "I've been walkin' *all day*. I had no idea Key West was so far.

"We wouldn't mind at all," I said quickly, "but the door is jammed and we have no way of getting into the camper. *No way!*"

"Oh," the little old lady said, "then I'll just pop into your station wagon. Let me off anyplace." With this she *did* pop into the station wagon before I could stop her.

"Say—*he's* naked!" she said, indicating the little gangster who was still hung up on the back of the front seat. "Why is he naked?"

"Because he doesn't have any clothes on," Reiko said. If logic was needed, Reiko could supply it.

"Oh," the little old lady said, and promptly nodded off.

"Now what do we do?" Reiko said.

"Nothing. When *they* go—*she* goes!"

I don't know whether any of you have ever tried to drive a car pulling a camper off a bridge, but it ain't easy. *Un*-jacknifing a camper with each futile try to get through the guard rail is extremely frustrating. When you turn the car wheels to the *left*, the camper goest *right*, and when you turn the car wheels *right*, the camper goes *left*, and when you don't turn the car wheel at *all*, the camper swings wide and wild and bashes in your headlights. You can't win.

156

I got the car and the trailer lined up again for another try for a suicide leap and was just about to tie down the gas pedal when I heard an ominous hum. What *now*, I thought—*killer bees?????*

I was wrong, the ominous hum grew to a tremendous roar of at least ten or twelve thousand motorcycles, all ridden by monsters dressed like Darth Vader, with large swastikas emblazoned on the sides of their black helmets! My God! Hitler is alive and well and crossing Lovers' Leap on his way to conquer Danbury!

I was sure they'd screech to a halt and wipe us out just for the hell of it, but they didn't. They kept on going like blazing furies, all except one of them. He stopped at the far end of the bridge and yelled, "Merry Christmas to all—and to all a 'good night.'" Then he gunned his Yamaha and careened into the swirling monsoon.

The little old lady awoke with a start. "What was that????"

"Christmas," Reiko said. "It's early this year."

The old lady jabbed the little gangster with her elbow. "You're *naked!*" she said, and went right back to sleep.

"Here comes somebody else," Reiko said, just as I was about to release our deadly catapult once again. "We'd better act like we're changing a tire or something. Somebody's liable to start asking questions."

I agreed with Reiko and grabbed the tools and started removing the lugs on the left rear wheel. I've never moved so quickly in my life.

And none too soon, because out of the darkness

157

and onto the bridge came tons of fat women—forty or fifty of them—jogging. "One, two, three, four. One, two, three, four." On and on. Lovers' Leap Bridge, which had been built in 1887 out of Civil War surplus, started to sway from side to side—slowly at first, then faster and wider.

"Break step!" I screamed just in time.

"What's the idea?" the chief lardo wanted to know.

"Didn't you feel the bridge?" Reiko asked her.

"I don't go round feeling bridges," the fat lady said. "And what business is it of yours, you little Filipino trouble-maker?"

"I'm Japanese," Reiko said. "Filipinos have funny eyes."

"She's right," I said. "Ask any soldier, you *always break step* when you *cross* a *bridge!*"

"What the hell's that got to do with it?" the fat lady wanted to know. "We're not soldiers, we're weight watchers."

"Then watch your weight when you're crossing bridges," Reiko said, "or you're liable to find yourself in a lot of rivers."

"Look," I said, suddenly reasoning through the mists of vodka, "it must be three o'clock in the morning. This is a helluva time to go jogging."

"I know," the fat lady said, "but when we jog in the daylight, everybody laughs because we hold onto our boobs."

"I don't understand," I said. "Why do you hold onto your . . . ?"

"If we don't hold onto our boobs when we jog, they fly up and around our necks. It feels like you're being mugged by a Polish sausage."

158

"Would you like a drink?" I said, offering her my half-filled bottle.

"You're goddamn right!" the fat lady said. "If I gotta watch my weight, I might as well be drunk so it won't bother me to watch what I'm watchin'."

"That's beautiful," I said, as the fat lady killed the rest of my vodka supply.

"Let's go, Fat Ladies!" the fat lady said, handing me back my bottle. "We gotta make Danbury before dawn. Ready! Set!—Hold your boobs!" And away they went. "Hup! Two! Three! Four! Hup! Two! Three! Four!" Fifty or sixty tons of fun.

They never did break step and the bridge swayed perilously until they reached the far side. It moaned and groaned, but U.S. Steel was watching over us and it didn't collapse.

"I hope that's the end of the traffic," Reiko said wearily. "I'm getting sleepy. Put the wheel back on and let's give it one more try."

"Okay," I said, giving the wheel a good bounce like the guy at the filling station always does. It seemed like fun and I bounced it again. This time it bounced right out of my hands and rolled across the bridge roadway and right under the guard rail and right down one thousand feet into the river.

"Now you've done it!" Reiko said, in the same tone that women have used on men since man and woman stopped grunting and started talking. They always make you feel like you've done something stupid on *purpose*. And it works! I felt exactly like I had been planning for months to remove a tire on the Lovers' Leap Bridge in the middle of the night and roll it off and into the river.

159

"For Crissakes," I yelled, "don't panic! We've got a spare!"

"Well, put it on and let's get going! It's starting to snow!"

"All right! All right! The spare just happens to be a snow tire—brand new—with nice long metal studs!" Which was, accidentally, the truth.

Time passed (at least twelve minutes) and I had the snow tire in place and I was just tightening the last lug when the law pulled up in an unmarked car with the exception of half a dozen flashing red and blue lights on its roof. It looked like Radio City on tour.

A very short State Trooper stepped out of the car. "Having trouble, folks?"

"Well, yes," I admitted.

"It's against the law to camp on a bridge," the trooper said.

"We weren't camping," Reiko said. "We were just changing a tire. Any law against *that*?"

"Well," the trooper said, "now that you mention it . . . "

"Holy Christ!" I said. "*Everything* is against the law!"

"Well," the trooper said, "now that you mention it. But let's not get into *that*. Just get that rig offa the bridge and we'll just forget the whole . . . Wait a minute!"

"What's the matter?" I cried. "I'll have it down off the jack in a couple of minutes and . . ."

"That's a *snow* tire!" The trooper was shocked.

"It's *snowing* !" Reiko said, reasonably.

"Sure it's snowing," the trooper said, "but it's May

160

second, two days after the legal date for removing snow tires and switching to regular tires!"

"But this is Connecticut," I argued, hopelessly. "The weather changes just like that!"

"Well," the trooper said, putting his little book back into his pocket, "I'll forget it this time, but next time . . ."

The trooper got back into his well-lit chariot and drove off. The two blondes in his back seat and one on the roof waved bye-bye to us.

"We better go home," Reiko said. "I can't keep my eyes open and this whole thing is hopeless. No matter what, we can't get through that guard rail."

I agreed and pumped the jack all the way down, but I still couldn't get it free.

"Goddamn jack," I muttered.

"It's not the jack," Reiko said. "It's the tire. It's flat."

It was then *I* had to be restrained from jumping off Lovers' Leap Bridge, without a lover.

Reiko grabbed me and calmed me down to the point where I could drive again, and we took off for home. Just as we were turning off the bridge and onto the highway, we heard a wild screeching of tires behind us, followed by the noise of tearing metal. We looked back just in time to see a little red Volvo go flying through the air and down into the depths of Lovers' Leap gorge.

Reiko and I looked at each other.

"Some people have all the luck," Reiko said.

Driving a heavy Buick station wagon with a flat left-rear tire and pulling a forty-foot super-camper was

161

like towing a seagoing oil rig out to the drilling site during the hurricane season. The drag was fearful and the noise had never been heard on this earth before.

As we turned down Heigh-ho Road and toward Herb Hagedorn's driveway, I thought we would see the whole neighborhood fleeing en masse, fearing an invasion by Martians or whatever they envisioned by the crashing, grinding clangor of our approach. But we saw no one.

By that time the left-rear wheel had lost its lovely brand-new snow tire. Its shreds littered the highway for miles, and the once perfectly round wheel was now an octagon, a hexagon, and a square. That it could have become all three was impossible, but the battering journey had somehow arranged it in this inconceivable configuration.

Going up Herb's driveway, we increased our decibel range above and beyond the realm of reasonability by the simple procedure of running over three tricycles and a wheelbarrow filled with recycleable beer cans left in the drive by the Hagedorn's three untidy children.

At dawn Reiko and I crawled into bed. Mrs. Ogelvie and the little gangster were back in their proper freezers. The little old lady back-packer had been removed from her forty winks and pointed in the direction of Key West and given a gentle shove. Herb Hagedorn's Buick station wagon and his forty-foot camper were exactly where he had left them in his driveway before they had been taken for an exciting evening on Lovers' Leap Bridge.

Everything was exactly as it was before, except that the only part of the car and camper that wasn't bent almost beyond recognition were Herb's car keys and his "Blow Your Horn For Jesus" bumper sticker.

CHAPTER

26

GETTING to sleep after our tilt with the Lovers'
Leap Bridge guard railing was almost impossible. I
tried Sominex, Nytol, Seconal, Dalmane, and seven
eighths of an ounce of pot [the legal limit (at our
house), for medicinal purposes]. Nothing helped. I
even tried closing my eyes and counting the veins in
the back of my lids. That didn't help either.

I had almost made it when suddenly I heard Herb
Hagedorn opening and slamming the doors of his
car. Here it comes, I thought, but I was wrong. He
was simply getting rid of two or three hundred Big
Mac burger cartons. The way he was getting rid of
them seemed more like a challenge than "Let's Be
Neat" week. Herb was shoveling the Big Mac cartons
out of the back of his station wagon and pitching
them over the fence into our wading pool. My first
impulse was to grab something lethal and rush out
there and dispatch him instanter, but my remaining
common sense stopped me.

I watched Herb do his dirty work for quite a few
moments, then as he finished, looking quite pleased
with himself, he went into his garage, brought out a
large can of Magic-Wax, and started waxing his car. I

couldn't believe it! There wasn't one square inch of that lovely Buick Estate Wagon that wasn't dented, crushed, gouged, augered, reamed, ripped, or breached by its traumatic treatment the night before, but Herb *waxed* the whole thing, then buffed it thoroughly with an electric device. None of this cosmetic craziness changed the Buick's ravaged looks one whit. It still looked like a car that had been sideswiped by a billion-gallon oil tanker and a Chicago River bridge swinging open at the same time, but Herb either didn't notice, or he was setting a trap.

He ignored completely the crumpled mass of super-camper which was still attached to the battered Buick.

"Is *he* crazy?" Reiko asked, crouching alongside me at the window.

"I think it's his sense of touch. I think God took it away from him for some sin. He's Catholic, you know. God really gives it to *them* if they stray."

"I know," Reiko said, "but if they confess they get a lollipop and a Pepsi."

That was close enough to the wine and the wafer so I let it go. If that's what she was getting at. (We'll never know.)

Once Herb had finished his waxing and buffing, he casually got into the car and drove off, never noticing, it seemed, that the left front wheel was rubbing against the fender and squealing like a stuck goat and blue smoke caused by the extreme friction was curling up and blowing right into Herb's open window. He coughed a little, but he didn't stop.

"My goodness," Reiko said, "he didn't even notice the noise or pay any attention to the smoke!"

165

"He noticed it all right," I said. "He's a Catholic, but when it's convenient he switches to Christian Science—so when your left front tire is rubbing against your bashed-in fender and emitting blue smoke, it's *not really happening.*"

"What about that left rear wheel? The square one? And *look!* He's running over the kid's tricycles and the wheelbarrow again!"

"Wow! Look at the sparks! It's like the Fourth of Julys we used to have in the old days."

"What if the car catches fire? And *he* catches fire? Does Christian Science allow you to notice *that!!!*"

"Yes. You're allowed to notice that, and if your car is equipped with a CB radio, you pick up the microphone and yell: 'Mayday!'"

"Mayday? What the hell is Mayday?" Reiko asked.

"I'm not quite sure, but school bus drivers always yell 'Mayday' when they're crossing the railroad tracks in New Jersey."

This seemed to satisfy Reiko, if not me. The strain of the two stiffs in the two freezers was getting to me. I knew that the best thing, in the beginning when we just had one stiff, would have been to go to the police and tell them the whole story. *Maybe* that would have been the best thing. To put myself in Chief Slocum's place—would *I* believe me! *No?* I certainly would *not!* Not after spending hours and weeks and months going around town *before* Mrs. Ogelvie accidentally deceased herself, telling everybody that I intended to become a murderer. I had even made up a story about taking a course, from the Famous Westport Murder by Mail Institute. I had an autographed pic-

166

ture of Jack the Ripper in my study, "To Jack from Jack, with admiration."

Then I saw a movie on television, "The Sam Shepherd Story." *That* convinced me how screwed up the evidence and lawyers and nutty witnesses can be. Sam could have been walking on the moon the *night* his wife was *murdered!* They *still* would have convicted him! And how about Sacco and Vanzetti? They were electrocuted for murder in 1927, and last week the Governor of Massachusetts proclaimed one day to be Sacco and Vanzetti Day, and everybody *honored* them with New England boiled dinners, weenie roasts, planting trees, and a few liquor store stick-ups. That case alone would have made me cautious because: *"The trial was sharply criticized by the Wickersham Commission on law procedure"* (a couple of weeks after the executioner had pulled the switch). "Hey, Nicola! Hey, Bartolomeo! Didja hear what Wickersham said about youse guys???? Youse guys didn't get a fair trial!!!!"

CHAPTER

27

AFTER Virgil, the welder, had once again sealed the tops of both freezers, without uttering a word, as he took my check and zoomed off into the night, I climbed the stairs to my study. Every writer has a study. *Study* is a euphemism for Golgotha—*a place of agony and sacrifice.*

At the moment I didn't plan any sacrifice, but I programmed myself for a little agony. I wanted to go over my past life bit by bit and try to fathom how I had gotten myself in my present predicament.

In my early years, my middle years, and down toward my Social Security (which I didn't feel was too social OR secure) I have tried many careers. Professional football player with the Lynbrook Tigers ($10.00 per game and all the cheerleaders you could catch. This wasn't too difficult because they were all unsteady divorçees with blue-rinsed hair and baggy pom-poms).

As a professional boxer I had thirteen minor bouts and one major catastrophe—an exhibition bout with Ben Jeby, who just happened to be the middleweight champion of the world (a fact no one had acquainted me with BEFORE I stepped into the ring with this slashing wildcat).

In Hollywood, I had been a movie chorus boy, a Busby Berkeley Boy. No one ever seems to remember that Buzz had boys, too (I mean to dance).

To sum it all up without too much ado, I had been everything but a Muppet (they never asked me), but I'd really never ever done anything to lead me down the path I was now following—almost but not quite—a *fugitive*. And I didn't like it. There was only one sensible thing to do. *How many times* had I told this to myself *before?*

I reached for the telephone and dialed the police station and quickly hung up. I didn't have the guts. Or the right story.

I started to make notes on murder. Or rather on murder *alibis*. Why did you do it, Leopold? Or Loeb? Or George Kratzmeyer? Well, I just don't know. *Something* came over me. Yeah, *that's it! Something came over me* and the next thing you know I went to Abercrombie & Fitch and bought this *twenty-seven-inch hunting knife and* stuck it in my *mother!* It just seemed like the *only thing* to *do*—at the *time.*

Or: I don't remember *anything!* I have these spells—like—you know—*amnesia.* I *black out* and then I don't remember *anything!.* I *could* have killed her. I *just don't know! Where* did I get that *hand grenade?* I *just don't know!* I wasn't in the war—so I couldn't have just *picked it up.* Maybe, maybe I bought it from a guy. *What* guy? I *just don't know!* Some guy at the ball park—he wasn't selling popcorn or beer—he was selling *hand grenades.* I *know* it doesn't make any sense, but nowadays *what does! What does?*

169

Or: I just found her in the bathtub— dead.

Shee-it! Nobody would believe THAT!

CHAPTER

28

THE baby, to whom we still hadn't given a name, got cuter with every passing day. We, as doting parents, felt this intensely. If anyone else felt this, we'll never know because who in their right mind is going to tell you the truth about your own child. Not even Doctor Spock. That is one of the reasons Doctor Spock is so successful, and one of the things I learned from reading his book *Baby and Child Care.* With him, *every* baby is *adorable,* which is one of the reasons this book sold over forty billion copies in seventy-six languages.

Doctor Spock has a *new* book (he found the time somehow) called *From Birth to Forty-six.* It takes the child right through his or her second year in high school.

The good Doctor wanted to call it, *From Potty to Pot,* but his publisher advised him that frivolity was not what was wanted these days. One had to be serious like *Star Wars* or the public wouldn't go for it. A baby book with a funny title might stop copulation dead, and the publisher would be stuck with forty billion copies of hardcover toilet paper (which would be difficult to fit into the average everyday type of holder).

171

After Mrs. Ogelvie had left us for a more convivial climate than Connecticut's, we had to rely on books and manuals and charts and pamphlets and anything else which would help guide us.

From the moment *we* started to take care of the baby, the slightest cough or sneeze or wind-breaking would send us to our extensive "baby library." We had baby books printed in Hindustani, Braille, Swahili, and Latin, so we could analyze wind-breaking in its pure, generic terms. We didn't want to know just *what* he was blowing— we wanted to know which Roman Emperor had blown it *first*.

From the beginning, it seemed that our baby contracted *every* known childhood malady. The first abnormal trait we noticed was that he did not suck his thumb. We looked this up in Doctor Smather's nine hundred and thirty-two page handy manual *The Thumb and Your Child*. There have been many cases where a child does *not* suck his thumb (as you can imagine in nine hundred and thirty-two pages). Most of these cases indicated nothing too harmful, but sometimes, according to Dr. Smathers, it pertained to a deficiency, mostly of something to suck. We tried lollipops. Nothing. We tried popsicles (seventeen flavors). Nothing. We tried a little blue baby blanket (the corner). Nothing. We tried Mrs. Ettinger's kid's thumb (she was the neighbor on the other side from Hagedorn's) and she had a new baby. Our baby liked this kid's thumb better than his own, but in time (two days) he had had enough. We thanked Mrs. Ettinger and gave her back her new baby.

There were times, many, many times when we wished that Mrs. Ogelvie hadn't gone and done what she had done. We missed her, especially when the baby started to cry. We knew we should keep calm, from reading Doctor Greenspan's book *How to Cure Your Baby of Infancy.* Doctor Greenspan wrote there are three reasons why a baby cries: (1) He's hungry. (2) He's wet. (3) He hates the people in the apartment upstairs (who aren't too fond of him either at three o'clock in the morning).

Sometimes, of course, it gradually dawned on us, that the baby cried because he had accumulated a large bubble inside of him and needed to be burped. I remember my very own mother told me (after I had grown up) that when *I* was a baby I had a *perpetual bubble* and she had to burp me almost continuously. Later *she* developed a little trouble, so I felt it was only fair thatI slung her over *my* shoulder and we took turns.

As the baby started to grow, he started to teethe. Just like all babies, his first tooth came as quite a surprise. I put my finger in his little mouth one Sunday morning and started feeling around and the next thing I knew, I was having a tetanus shot.

Reiko grew more confident as time passed and the baby was still alive and kicking (on the outside, now, of course), so she began to feed him baby food.

Giving the baby his first baby food (which comes in tiny jars) took a lot of guts on her part, because every tiny jar had a label warning that if you are giving your baby this particular baby food for the first time, the baby may get some unexpected reaction like a rash or nausea—or fits. In order to bolster Reiko's morale and courage, we invented a name for this new baby-food game; we called it Gerber's Roulette.

173

We'd use six different tiny jars of baby food—five were empty and the sixth was loaded.

A new baby book we'd just bought (we bought them all), Doctor Alvin Grumple's: *Your Baby's Bowels and How to Get More Joy Out of Them,* advised that nothing bothers some babies except milk. They're *allergic.* Then you have to get into formulas, or to be more exact—the *right* formula, which of course is *mission impossible.*

When trying to concoct the *right formula,* you have to try different *combinations* of, it seems, *everything!*

We *tried everything,* and just as we were about to give up we tried *one final batch,* consisting of one pound of powdered goat's milk, a Christmas fruitcake, and just a pinch of Seconal (not more than a spoonful). You put this in a Waring Mixer for two days (at half speed), then warm it, pound it into a bottle, and cap it with an eight-hole nipple and give it to your precious offspring. It worked fine with our baby: he went *right* to sleep. And for three days.

If you'd like to try this formula on *your* baby, here's a warning. Make sure your baby is not allergic to eight-hole nipples. It gives some babies such a feeling of overwhelming abundance that when they grow up they won't be satisfied with anything except Dolly Parton.

CHAPTER

29

THE phone had been ringing for at least six minutes. Reiko was asleep. The baby was asleep. The cat was asleep. The dog was asleep. The canary was also asleep, so it looked like it was up to me.

"Hello" I said, "Best little whorehouse in Texas."

"What????" The voice on the other end was aghast.

"What do you like?" I said. "Blondes, brunettes, redheads, black, brown, streaked—blue-rinsed?"

"I was kinda set on a case of Cutty Sark." It was the clown from Omaha (I was awake now).

"You know," I said, "you must be running up a new record for wrong numbers."

"This a whorehouse in Texas?"

"No," I said, "and not in Omaha either. We're in Connecticut—"

"Blondes, brunettes, redheads, black, brown, streaked and . . . ?"

"No, no," I said. "It's just that you woke me up."

"What about my case of Cutty Sark?" the Omaha voice said. "Got a big party comin' up tomorrow night—wedding—sort of unusual—too. I don't know what happened, but the best man is marrying the groom."

I hung up. I had enough problems in the *real* world.

"Who were you talking to at five o'clock in the morning this morning?" Reiko wanted to know, with a modicum of patience.

"A guy in Omaha."

"Oh." This was typical of my conversations with Reiko. I didn't know it then, but the pattern was being set. She no more cared about who I was talking with at five o'clock in the morning than she cared where the letter carrier spent his two weeks' vacation. But she had to ask.

"He's a guy with a wrong number in Omaha, Nebraska, who ordered a case of whiskey. He just called to find out what happened."

Reiko had left the living room and gone into the kitchen to see what she could do with rice that day. I addressed most of this last sentence to our dog, whom we, after careful thought, had named "Dog." Dog left the room before I had finished talking, and someone was knocking on our front door, using our impossibly large and ornate iron door knocker which we had placed there in hopes that it would make our flimsy middle-class front door look like it had been imported from Beverly Hills.

As it turned out, this gauche, outsized, solid-iron door knocker had never been used as it was supposed to be. That is to let us know, *lightly* with a *gentle* tap tap, that our friendly neighborhood aluminum-siding salesman wished a word with us. Everyone, it seemed, thought that it was an ancient battering ram, and that the only way they would gain access to the inner re-

176

cesses of our cozy cottage would be to use this metallic device to hammer the front door until it collapsed. Or someone opened it.

I opened it. As usual I was expecting at least the National Guard who would take me away in chains, but thank heaven I was wrong. This time. In place of the Guard stood a female (an assumption on my part)—a female with a voice heavy from too many long nights at Hurley's Bar. The voice said, "Hello—I'm your Avon lady."

It wasn't the Avon lady of television. It wasn't even close. It was a crone. A double-crone. Instead of one wart, she had two—like a matched pair. On either side of her nose. A nose I am sure she used moonlighting for ants. I could not believe this creature had been sent by Mr. Avon.

"I usedta be with Diane Von Furstenberg, but we had a falling out," the crone advised me.

"Oh?" I said, then trying to fill in what promised to be a pause, "Over money, I suppose?"

"No," the crone replied, giving her impossible nose a two-way wipe, "she was jealous."

I was dying to know why, but for the first time in my garrulous life I said nothing. But I soon realized I didn't have to.

"Yeah," the crone said, tidying up her nose once again, "I got this drip," she explained, then continuing, "She was jealous because men used to stare at me on the street."

"Oh," I said again, "well, we . . . er . . ."

"Is the lady of the house in—*Mrs.* Ogelvie?"

"Oh, I'm not *Mr.* Ogelvie. I just live here. I mean, my name is Douglas. Mrs. Ogelvie is . . . Well, she's our baby's nurse, or I should say—I should *definitely* say—she *was* our baby's nurse and she . . . well . . . she's not with us anymore."

"Oh," the crone said. "Who's she with now?"

"It's hard to say," I managed.

"You must have given her a letter of recommendation. What name? I mean who did you address the letter to?"

"Oh, yes. To whom it may concern, I believe it said. Yeah, that's it. 'To whom it may concern.' "

The subject seemed definitely closed with this, but the crone—her name turned out to be Miss Dern—somehow was inside the house. She must have slipped past me while I was looking right at her. I suddenly found myself following her into our living room (she *knew* where it was) and her bags of samples were, as if by some other magic, spread and open all over the living room floor.

"Is there a *Mrs.* Douglas?" Miss Dern wanted to know by this time. I was wondering, too—what the hell happened? Where was Reiko when I needed her? Here I am trapped alone and helpless with the Wart Fairy.

"We have cosmetics for men, too, you know," Miss Dern said, holding up a phallic (aren't they all?) lipstick container.

"I haven't used lipstick since I went to Harvard," I said.

"The Hasty Pudding Club?" she asked.

"No," I said, and that concluded that dandy conversation piece.

"How about baby powder? It comes in all shades, you know—white, brown, yellow, and black."

"I'll take a quart of black," I said. Where the hell was Reiko?

"You'll never regret it," Miss Dern said. "You'll look just like Harry Belafonte. Just unbutton your shirt a little."

Reiko entered.

"Ah," Miss Dern exclaimed, "and who is this cute little Jap?"

"She's a Kamikaze pilot I knew during the war," I explained. "We were in the same squadron together."

"How nice," Miss Dern said. "I do wish you knew where Mrs. Ogelvie is now, or where she'll be, like say—next week. She was one of my best customers."

"I'm sure she still is," Reiko said. "What is it you're selling?"

"This is the Avon lady," I said by way of explanation.

"My God!" Reiko said.

"I know how you feel," Miss Dern said. "People never expect a woman of my position and station in life to be selling Avon products, but—ever since the Prince died . . ."

"What Prince?" Reiko and I both said simultaneously.

"Valiant," Miss Dern said.

This gave us something to think about.

We bought everything she had, including her carrying cases, just to get rid of her, but just as she was leaving and very happy at having had the best day of her Avon career, she spied Mrs. Ogelvie's knitting bag on top of the coffee table—very apparent were the needles and her half-finished pair of winter snuggies she had been making when she . . .

"Look!" Miss Dern almost shrieked. "Gladys's knitting bag! She's coming back! She's coming back!"

We were speechless for a moment, then Reiko half whispered, "How do you know she's coming back?"

"She would never leave her knitting bag *anywhere* if she weren't *coming back!* And look! *Snuggies!* She's going to need these soon!"

Reiko and I just looked at each other as Miss Dern twirled gaily out the door and into the night and the warm Caribbean rain (which just happened to be falling in Connecticut at the moment).

CHAPTER

30

"HOW the hell did we ever miss Ogelvie's knitting bag? Right in the middle of the living room coffee table—with her *snuggies hanging out?*" I was almost *hysterical* again.

"What are we gonna do with all this Avon stuff?" Reiko asked, in the same tone she used when she thought about cleaning up the attic for once and for all! (We *never* cleaned up the attic, but we thought about it for many years.)

"Give it to the poor," I suggested.

"There are *no poor* in Old New Litchridge!" Reiko reminded me, sounding like Rose Kennedy.

"The IRS isn't finished yet," I reminded her.

"Well," Reiko said, bored with the subject, "I'll never use this black baby powder. Who can we give *that* to?"

"How much black baby powder we buy?"

"The large economy size—ten pounds—and there's a prize in there somewhere like Crackerjacks."

"You'd look like a coal miner before you found it."

"You're not supposed to *look* for it. It's not like *Treasure Island.* You're supposed to just use the baby powder until you *get* to the prize."

"I'd be eager. I'd look," I said. And I *would*, too. Ten pounds of black baby powder. Who the hell did we know who had a black baby?

Most of my black show business friends had married honkies and they didn't have any *black* kids. Too bad we didn't buy ten pounds of Avon mocha. Or *cafe au lait*.

"I've got seventy-six shades of lipstick and I don't care for any of them," Reiko moaned. "What will I do with *them*?"

"If they're waterproof, we can go down to the subway yards and spend our weekends writing graffiti all over the cars like everybody else does."

"I doubt if we could find a subway car that hasn't already been graffitied."

She was right, I thought, and we couldn't compete in artistry with some of the *real talent* they've got living close to the yards. The Long Island subway car yards are surrounded by at least five thousand Porno Picassos.

Their more ambitious spectacles have used up all the space on full trains already coupled for a run. Some of Pablo's penises are eight and ten cars long! Sliding into the tunnel under Park Avenue could furnish one with a suddenly startling panorama.

"Look *at that*!" one of my South Bronx friends said, "New York's gettin' *screwed again*!"

We finally decided that our newly acquired and vast supply of Avon products had better be saved and kept on hand for Miss Dern. We were sure the Avon Crone would be back for re-orders and we would

182

have to prove that we hadn't *run out* as yet and *never would!*

Our attic inventory increased a hundredfold in one night. We'd never be able to dig out now.

Our electric bill rose alarmingly. Two deep freezers plugged in at the same time and set for way below zero seemed to inspire our electric meter to greater glory than it had ever known.

The meter reader noticed this, and he became quite friendly—a side of his personality we had never noticed before. But *now* we were *big-time spenders!*

"You folks sure know how to live!" were some of his friendly words. We had no way of knowing what he meant until we got that first monthly bill—pushed to a new high by our freshly acquired portable mauso-leum.

"I don't know," Reiko said one dinnertime, be-tween trying to shove pablum into the baby's nose (that's where most of it was going) and trying to get me to eat my spinach and raw fish. "Maybe we should hire a lawyer and let him take care of everything."

"And just who would *that* be?" I said in a manner that in no way could be interpreted as agree- able.

"How about Terry Collins?" Reiko said.

"You mean the guy who *helped* us when we had a real-estate problem and charged us a hundred and twenty-five dollars for a phone call and got a *wrong number* and *never told us?*"

"All right, all right," Reiko said, still softly, which

was unusual. "Who are we going to get that we can trust?"

"You're supposed to be able to trust *any* lawyer."

"Yes," Reiko agreed, "but we're not talking about Grimm's Fairy Tales, we're talking about *like it is!*"

"Well, let's forget about *lawyers* then," I said.

"You want to try the Lovers' Leap Bridge again?"

"I don't think so."

"Herb's got his car all fixed up. It looks great and runs great."

"Yeah, but I went over the bridge the other day and they've reinforced it some more. Nothing would go through that guard rail now except a Sherman tank."

"They got a Sherman tank down on the Village Green. I don't know how it runs, but it sure looks pretty—it's all painted up. They just painted it last week."

"I know," I said. "I saw it, but that's a war memorial. I'm sure they don't have an engine in it anymore, and if it did, it takes a helluva lot of gas or whatever they use in Sherman tanks, and, Jesus, is it noisy! We could never sneak it off the Green and down the road to the bridge."

"Yeah. And people would ask us where Mrs. Ogelvie learned how to drive a Sherman tank."

"That's easy. We'd just tell them she learned in Africa in World War II—the German Army. She was known as the Desert Fox!"

"That was *Rommel!*"

"Right!—Her *maiden* name."

There was a long silence after this, broken only by the sound of woodpeckers pecking off the shingles on

184

all four corners of the house. They were drilling away like it was a contest.

"We have to do something about those woodpeckers," Reiko said.

"Yeah," I said. "They're *hungry!*"

"This is the first time they've ever eaten the shingles at night. I wonder if that *means* anything?" Reiko was into some kind of Oriental scene where everything that happened meant something else. For instance, woodpeckers eating a house at night seemed (to her) to have some special voodoo-type significance. To me it meant only that they were bored and couldn't sleep.

The telephone was ringing again.

"Who could that be? It's almost ten o'clock," Reiko said.

"It's the woodpeckers. They need more shingles."

"Hello," Reiko said cautiously. Then there was a long pause. Finally, "It's the Chief of Police, Captain Slocum. You better talk to him—"

What the hell was I going to say? I wasn't a very good liar except in a favorable circumstance—like a New Year's Eve Party in a Mental Hospital.

"Hello, Chief, what can I do for you?" (A nice original opening).

"Jack, I got a problem," the Chief said.

"You too?" I said, with a jollity so phony it could be detected by a three-year-old retarded baboon.

"What?" the Chief said.

"What's your problem?"

"Well, actually, I'd like to come up and talk to you about it."

"Tonight?"

"No, it can wait."

"Good."

"How about six—tomorrow morning?"

"Oh," I said. "Yeah, that'll be fine. I'll just take a short nap and see you then."

The Chief of the Old New Litchridge Police hung up.

I took three Seconals and was awake all night.

CHAPTER

31

CHIEF Slocum of the Old New Litchridge Police Department arrived a lot later than he had suggested the night before, which gave us a lot more time to get exceedingly nervous.

"Jack," Chief Slocum said, "I'll get straight to the point."

"That's the best way," I said. "I got four television shows and a magazine article to write before lunchtime."

"Gee," the Chief said, "I'd like to get on one of those talk shows sometime and tell 'em what really happens in New Old Litchridge—especially on weekends."

"I don't think they'd go for that kind of stuff—on talk shows. They're pretty fussy, except maybe late at night."

"Late at night's okay with me," the Chief said.

"What was your problem?" I said. I felt if anything horrendous was going to happen it might as well happen right here and now.

"It's *your* problem," the Chief said. Here it comes, I thought. I resisted the urge to hold out my wrists for the handcuffs or throw myself up against the wall with my legs spread so he could feel my crotch for hidden weapons, all the while nostalgically thinking that my crotch hadn't hidden a weapon since my senior year at Hollywood High.

"It's your neighbors," the Chief continued. "They've been complaining about that big truck in your driveway. You know—you got it loaded with deep freezers—they been complaining that it's spoiling the tone of the whole neighborhood."

Reiko and I both sighed heavily. The Chief misunderstood this.

"I know how you feel," the Chief said, "like you're being harassed by the police. Well, unfortunately, we got an ordinance in Old New Litchridge: no loaded trucks in private driveways for more than three days."

"That's crazy!" Reiko said.

"Did you ever get a good look at the Selectmen we got here in Old New Litchridge? They've passed more kooky ordinances than they got in downtown Outer Mongolia." I didn't understand this last, but I presumed that downtown Outer Mongolia was a mixed-up mess.

"I gotta give you a summons," the Chief continued. "And you gotta get that truck and those freezers out of your driveway by tomorrow night."

I was truly relieved, but I thought I'd throw in a few objections to make it all look real. "What about our neighbors with those enormous Winnebago house campers blocking their driveways and most of the time hanging over onto the sidewalks. Kids can't even ride their bikes—they keep bumping into somebody's portable toilet."

188

"Yes," Reiko chimed in, "and what about those cabin cruisers? Everybody around here seems to have one and they're parked forever in their driveways. They hang over into the sidewalks and even *into the street,* and then the kids can't even ride their bikes in the *streets* because they're liable to get a skull fracture from a protruding dinghy! What about *them?????*"

"Unfortunately," the Chief said, "the Selectmen didn't pass any ordinance against *them.*"

"Because *they're* the ones with the *Winnebagos* and the *cabin cruisers!*"

"Looks that way," the Chief admitted. "But, like JFK said, it's an unfair world. LBJ said it, too."

"Yeah," Reiko agreed, "even Hirohito said it."

"You're kidding," I said. "When was that?"

"Right after Jimmy Doolittle bombed his goldfish."

"Poor goldfish," I said.

"Yeah, Hirohito wrote a poem about it."

"He always writes poems," the Chief said.

"Right," Reiko said. "This was a sad poem."

"A sad poem—about goldfish????? What was it called?"

"Jimmy Doolittle—You Son-of-a-bitch," Reiko said.

Early the next morning, we were awakened by a loud pounding on the door. It's the Avon lady again, I thought, as I wrapped myself in an old Hudson's Bay blanket (which Reiko had fashioned into a bathrobe for me back in the days when she was actually sewing instead of talking about it).

I couldn't find my Louis XIV bedroom slippers, so I lit a cigarette instead. I don't smoke, but my feet

189

were cold and this seemed like the only sensible thing to do.

Reiko wasn't at my side when I approached the front door. She was still in bed, dreaming about Sessue Hayakawa. The man I saw through our little safety peephole was a police officer. One I had never seen before in Old New Litchridge.

I unlocked the four burglar-proof locks we had on the door, one of which fell off and crashed to the floor as its screws tore out of the solid teak of which our safety door was supposedly constructed.

The police officer was at least eight feet tall, it seemed in my early-morning rheumy eyes. "Mr. . . . er." He was consulting a little crumpled notebook. Then he found what he was looking for. "Mr.—er—Pennyfeather?"

"I—don't think so," I said. The police officer was so tentative, I wasn't quite sure either.

"Isn't this 429 Horse Hollow Road, Old New Litchridge, Connecticut?"

"No," I managed to deny. "This is 426 Heigh-ho Road, Old New Litchridge, Connecticut—" I added, indefinitely.

"Oh," the police officer said, and flipped through a few more pages of his disgraceful note pad. Then he started all over again. He left out the part where he pounded on the door, but he started right at the beginning.

"Mr. Jack—Douglas—426 Heigh-ho Road, Old New Litchridge, Connecticut 06899?"

"Right," I said, swallowing a nervous yawn and scratching my rear *thoroughly* (we had a goose down

190

mattress with the feathers all running in the same direction. It was like sleeping on a bed of slanted shingle nails. If one moved down during the night—one could be raked as if by tigers).

"You got fleas?" the police officer wanted to know.

"Yeah," I said, not wishing to start trouble. "I have to wear a flea belt. It discourages ticks and vampire bats, too."

The police officer looked a long hard look at me after this.

"Would you like a cup of Irish coffee," I asked the large cop, who looked like he could have been Irish or at least a Neanderthal from near Dublin.

"When did you last see the *late* Chief Slocum of the Old New Litchridge Police Force?" he asked abruptly.

"The *late*—?"

"Yeah, he was found on top of an old mattress out at the dump about eleven o'clock last night. When did you last see the late Police Chief Charles M. Slocum?"

Jesus! I thought. I hope *I* wasn't the *last* to see him. But how could I be? He had been here quite early in the morning and I was sure he had left before noon. Quite a while before noon. But, instead of just answering the question, I *had* to *elaborate*.

"I hope you don't think *I* had anything to do with . . ."

"With *what?*"

"With . . ." I stopped. I felt as if I *did* have something to do with his demise, if that's what he was—demised.

"With his *murder?* Is *that* what you were going to say?" The big cop was getting a little unfriendly.

191

"Wait a minute, old buddy," I said. "If you're gonna adopt this third-degree tone of voice, I'm gonna call somebody."

"Call anybody you like," the big cop said. "Do you know your rights?" The cop pulled out a little card and started to read, "You will meet a tall, dark gypsy who will direct you to your fortune of gold, silver, diamonds and . . . Oh, shit!" He pulled out another card and read me my rights, which I knew by heart from television.

"Look," I said, "let's get this over with. I saw Charlie Slocum before noon yesterday. He left here long before lunch. He said something about getting a haircut and that's all I know."

"Here's something you *don't* know," the big cop smirked. "*You* and your *wife* were the last persons to see Charles Slocum *alive!*—*Think* about that. Just—*think* about that!" He slapped his filthy little notebook shut and was gone.

I thought about it. I thought about it a *long time!*

CHAPTER

32

I THOUGHT about"we were the last people to see Charlie Slocum alive" until Reiko finally conceded that morning had come, and no matter what, she *had* to get up.

"Who was that?" Reiko said, a cup of coffee in her hand, a cigarette in her mouth, and her hip-length hair piled on top of her head like black laundry.

"The pounding on the door?"

Reiko puffed another puff, all the while just tolerating me. She wasn't at her congenial best in the A.M.

"It was a big tough cop and Chief Slocum is dead."

"Did you tell him, 'Sorry, our deep freezers are full?'"

So that's the way it was going to be—the early morning Wide World of Sports for the bickering championship of Old New Litchridge.

"Yeah," I said, "I told him our quota of stiffs was full this month—try again next month."

"Was Charlie Slocum killed?"

"Jesus H. Christ! No, he wasn't *killed*. He just happened to be taking a nap out in the village dump and unfortunately he lay down on a *poisoned mattress!*"

"How could anybody poison a mattress?"

"Look, Charlie Slocum isn't *our* problem. It's *his*. He's dead and that's that! But apparently he was killed, and the police get very goddamn mad when one of *them* gets it. They're not going to give up until they find out who did it!" And this was indeed the truth—even in a little town like Old New Litchridge they had some very good cops and excellent detectives, and if Reiko and I were the last people to see Charlie Slocum alive, (which seems very strange) we were in big trouble. They'd be back again and again, asking questions until they figured out some kind of an answer, and here we were with two bodies parked in our driveway. Something had to be done! Gladys Ogelvie and the little crook with the big hard-on had to go!

"Why don't we try having a swimming pool put in, and after the hole is dug, we'll bury them—just a little deeper. Then after the cement is poured, who's going to find 'em?" This was Reiko's suggestion.

"I don't know," I said, "there's an awful lot of *ledge* around here."

"Jack, you know, and I know, from living in Connecticut that the ledge *isn't everywhere*. Lots of places, especially around Old New Litchridge, have swamp—even on the tops of hills. We've got a soft spot over near that big pine on the north side of our property. I'm sure there's no ledge there."

I thought about this. I knew things were getting too hot for us. We already had a summons to get the truck out of the driveway, and we certainly didn't want the cops towing it away, which they certainly

194

would do if we ignored the summons—and now this Chief Slocum thing.

I agreed. We'd give the swimming pool ploy a try.

The two freezers had been unwelded again, and the hole for our new swimming pool had been dug and shaped, and the down payment was safely put away in Blue Heaven Swimming Pool Company's bank account.

It was midnight. The witching hour. Mrs. Ogelvie, frozen stiff and naked, was sitting on the edge of the newly dug Blue Heaven Swimming Pool hole.

Alongside Mrs. Ogelvie we placed the nude little hood, his seemingly permanent erection pointing stiffly heavenward. (Which may have been a sign.) They made an uncharming couple as they patiently waited to be buried under our new fifteen-thousand dollar Blue Heaven swimming pool. Tomorrow the workmen would tie in the criss-cross of steel bars and cover them, Gladys Ogelvie, and little Max—with eight inches of gunnite, which would last longer and be a safer haven than the tombs of the Egyptian Pharaohs.

Reiko and I bought shovels in *New Jersey* so no one could trace them to *us*. We had both worn mustaches and given the hardware people phony names. *Why* they wanted our names we never learned, but apparently in New Jersey you can buy a Saturday Night Special without *any* identification at all. A shovel, however, was different. They *had* to know what you were going to use it for. We told them we were going to bury a couple of dead gangsters (I couldn't resist this) and they gave us the shovels without further

195

ado. Burying dead gangsters in chicken yards was a way of life in New Jersey. It wasn't *all* riding to hounds with Jackie O.

Our plan, of course, was certainly not new. It had been used for years by various nefarious characters to get rid of their victims.

Reiko and I got down in the soft dirt of the bottom of our newly dug swimming pool. We didn't dare use any flashlights or lanterns, which I'm sure would have attracted the neighborhood watchdog, Herb Hagedorn. He would have been over immediately, either asking questions or helping us. Neither of which we wanted for this particular task.

The digging was easy. We were very pleased with ourselves. It was like playing in a sandpile or digging at the beach to build castles. In no time at all we were down about one foot. *Twin holes.* One foot deep, three feet wide, and six feet long. Then it bappened. Or I should say, two things happened. Herb Hagedorn was down at the bottom of the swimming pool with his shovel *helping* us, and we struck rock. *Solid ledge.* In every direction. We probed and dug and cursed, but that was it. Connecticut. The Nutmeg State. The Solid Ledge State. You had a choice in Connecticut. Solid rock ledge or deep, gooey swamp.

"Who are they?" Herb Hagedorn wanted to know, referring to the two dark figures sitting patiently at the edge of the rim of the pool hole.

"They waiting to swim?"

"Yeah," I said. "Herb, thanks for helping us make the pool deeper. We don't know what we would do if we didn't have you for a neighbor."

"Shucks," Herb said, like Mickey Rooney after Ann

196

Rutherford grabbed his balls in *Andy Hardy Takes a Warm Bath and Finds Himself.* "What are neighbors for?"

"So you're wondering, too," Reiko said. She said it so straight and deadpan that Herb laughed.

"Boy!" Herb said. "Jack, you got a gem here," referring to Reiko and trying to sneak in a little pinch. "A gem. She says such funny things and people never know whether she's kidding or not."

Reiko broke Herb's pinky and he left, nodding "goodnight" to the two silent figures still patiently sitting by the edge of the far from completed pool.

"Well," Reiko said, as we closed the freezers, which somehow, and with many near hernias, we had managed to move off the U-Drive and into a small room in back of the house, which we called a root cellar. I don't know why, but almost every house in New England had a root cellar, and not once did I ever see a root in any of them. We used ours for old rubber boots, skis, perpetually wet, greenish, moldy winter underwear, hundreds of discarded ripped and ragged old sweaters, tons of moth balls, moths, and now our two deep freezers.

"Fifteen thousand dollars right down the toilet," Reiko said, after we had filled in our unsatisfactory graves and hidden our New Jersey shovels in back of a false-fronted spice pantry we had in our old New England kitchen.

"I wouldn't say down the toilet," I said. "We'll get to use the swimming pool for a couple of weeks in August. With luck—maybe *three* weeks."

Reiko's non-delicate Japanese-doll reply was a loud, juicy Bronx cheer.

197

She was right, of course. The weather in Connecticut could be compared to the weather in California. *Predictable.* In California you could always count on a long, hot, dry summer followed by a long, hot, dry winter and Bob Hope's and Zsa Zsa Gabor's houses burning down. And California was always calling in thousands of little Indian fire fighters from Arizona and New Mexico.

These thousands of little Indians from Arizona and New Mexico, who got $7.50 an hour to fight the California forest fires every year, didn't perform rain dances. Rain dances prayed for rain. The thousands of little Indians from Arizona and New Mexico had a special dance—they prayed for careless smokers. That $7.50 an hour was a helluva lot more money than they could ever make herding goats. In Arizona or New Mexico. Or anywhere.

The Connecticut weather was just as Mark Twain said it was. Mark said, "If you don't like the weather now, just wait a minute." And he was right. In Connecticut you can get sun, moon, rain, hail, snow, and whale piss all within fifteen minutes. The whale piss only if the wind is blowing off Long Island Sound when a school of them are going south to spawn.

I felt maybe we should call the whole thing off and let our swimming pool deposit go, but then this might cause suspicion, which was something we didn't need any more of at the moment.

Especially after the next day when Herb Hagedorn let *everybody* in town know that the night before—we had been digging holes in our hole.

CHAPTER

33

THE baby, who was beginning to recognize us as his mother and father, had taken almost a full bottle when the telephone rang.

"What time tonight?" a voice asked. I thought it was the clown from Omaha calling for his case of booze.

"Oh," I said, "isn't it there yet?"

"Isn't *what where?*" the voice wanted to know.

"The case of booze you ordered about *two weeks* ago. I guess it was."

"I don't even drink," the voice yelled indignantly. "Who *is* this *anyway?*"

It began to trickle through that I didn't have the man from Omaha on the other end. "This is Jack Douglas. To whom am I speaking?"

"To *whom* are you speaking? To Mrs. *J. Walter Ferguson,* that's *to whom* you are speaking, and I am the President of the Old New Litchridge *Women's Christian Temperance Union.*"

"Good," I said. "And to *whom* would you like to *speak* with?"

"What the hell are you," Mrs. J. Walter Ferguson said, "some kinda English Composition nut?"

"No," I said. "Mrs. J. Walter Ferguson, you'll never

believe this, but I'm . . . I am a *minister* of the *gospel.* 'Let the words of my mouth, and the meditation of my heart, be always acceptable in thy sight—'" (I happened to have a copy of *The Prayer Book for Soldiers and Sailors* next to the phone, so I ad libbed out of it.) This didn't impress Mrs. J. Walter Ferguson one bit.

"Look, you crazy religious sonofabitch, let me talk to Mrs. Ogelvie!"

Oh, God!—*Now what?* Another of Gladys Ogelvie's long lost relatives?

"I'm sorry, but she's . . . er . . . busy right now. I think she's taking a bath."

"Well," Mrs. J. Walter Ferguson said, "may I leave a message?" Her tone was much softer now.

"Of course," I said. "I'll be sure and give it to her. That is if I ever see her."

"What?"

"*When* I see her," I corrected myself hastily, "I'll give her *any* messages *whatsoever.* Now—*what* is the *message?*"

"Just tell her," Mrs. J. Walter Ferguson said, blandly now, "just tell her that the Old New Litchridge Occult and Bridge Club will meet at the usual time tonight, eight o'clock, for our bi-monthly seance. Dear Mrs. Ogelvie, she is our only connection with our dear departed loved ones."

I repeated this, "Just tell Mrs. Ogelvie that the Old New Litchridge Occult and Bridge Club will hold a seance tonight at the usual time—eight o'clock—She is your only connection with your dear departed loved ones. Where? Mrs. Ferguson? *Where* will this take place, so I can *tell Mrs.* . . . ?"

"At the Douglas house, 426 Heigh-ho Road, where

she works. At eight o'clock. Thank you." Mrs. J. Walter Ferguson hung up.

I immediately looked up her name in the telephone directory. Mrs. J. Walter Ferguson had an *unlisted* number.

"My God!" I said. "My God! My God! My God!"

"The baby took almost a whole bottle tonight," Reiko said. I just grunted.

"The baby took almost a whole bottle," Reiko said again. "Doesn't that *mean* anything to you????" Reiko was highly incensed at my seeming indifference.

"Reiko, darling" I said,"it means everything to me, but put the *baby* back into his little *crib* and get Mrs. Ogelvie out of the *freezer!*"

"What!!!"

"I said"—my voice sounded like I was being hanged—"forget the baby!—Get Mrs. Ogelvie out of the freezer!"

"Have you gone bananas?????"

"Yes! Yes! Yes!" I was frothing, I felt. "Mrs. Ogelvie has to attend a meeting tonight."

"What??? Where?????"

"*Here*, that's *where!* Now come on. Get some of her clothes and let's get her out of the freezer. We got to get her dressed and ready by eight o'clock. That's in exactly *forty-six minutes!*"

Well—we did it. We got Mrs. Ogelvie out of the freezer, stiff as a board, and we got her into a muu-muu. A pink and blue muu-muu with "Keep Cool with Coolidge" written on the front of it. We got her propped up at one end of our dining room table. The end that was practically in the dark, because we light-

201

ed the dining room bycandlelight. And *very few* candles.

Remembering a seance Mrs. Ogelvie had conducted at our house in the past, we knew, thank God, that the other members of the Old New Litchridge Occult and Bridge Club communicated with their beloveds (who had passed on) through Mrs. Ogelvie, so *we* had to be *ready!*

I rigged a loudspeaker, a very small one that I had once used in my night club act, onto her lap. Her voice, which *I* was going to imitate, would sound like it was coming from her Antarctic crotch, but this could not be helped. I had no time for Senssurround.

"How about some music?" Reiko suggested.

"From *there?!*" I said. "You'd get an *echo.*"

"I just thought it would be appropriate," Reiko said. "You know—background music, like in the movies."

"Look," I said, "I've only got one small speaker, and I've gotta use that to answer questions."

Reiko didn't understand any of what we were getting at. She didn't know what a seance was.

"Mrs. Ogelvie is going to talk to the dear departed of Old New Litchridge. She's the only one around here that knows how to do it! Don't you remember that meeting they had here one Thursday night?"

"She's going to talk to the dear departed?"

"Yes."

"How's she gonna do that when she's departed herself?" Reiko snorted on this one.

"I'm gonna do it!"

"You're *kidding!*"

"No, I'm not, I'm *desperate!*" I said, and I *was*. "I'm

going to hide behind the curtains with this hand mike, and whatever the Old New Litchridge Occult and Bridge Club wants to know—or whomever they want to talk to in heaven—or wherever they are. *I'm* going to *answer* them—through Mrs. Ogelvie's crotch."

"I'd like to talk to my dear departed husband," one member of the Old New Litchridge Occult and Bridge Club said. She was a dumpy little woman who seemed to think that the late hats of Mary, late Queen Mother of England, were still making it big. And maybe they were, for all I knew. (There was very little about current fashion in *Boy's Life* magazine.) I became so fascinated, like a bird and a snake, with her hat I almost didn't respond. And when I did gather myself together I giggled a little.

"I don't think it's funny, Gladys," the exotic-hatted dumpy little lady said. "I don't think it's funny at all. Mr. Zok was a good man."

"Mr. *Zok!*" Now I *really* giggled, although I knew she wasn't making up this name. I had seen it on a mailbox somewhere in the vicinity of Camelot Acres. Camelot Acres was the name of a cluster development which constantly made headlines in the Old New Litchridge *News,* because Camelot Acres had a septic system which made headlines. The Camelot Acres septic system kept *flooding out* Ye Olde Heritage Retirement Home and Discotheque—the cluster development across the road.

Finally, Ye Olde Heritage Retirement Home and Discotheque had a large bulletin board erected in front of its main entrance like a marquee, and every

203

other day except during the cold months it spelled out in bold five-foot-high neon letters—SHIT ON AGAIN!

Mrs. Zok repeated her request. "I would like to talk to my dear departed husband. I have a very important question to ask him!"

I was controlled by now, and ready for any important question Mrs. Zok wanted to ask the late Mr. Zok. "Yes, my dear," I spoke in a voice similar to Mrs. Ogelvie's. Mrs. Ogelvie was the go-between between the going and the gone.

"What is it you would like to know and how are the children?"

Mrs. Zok was about to answer when she stopped in mid-breath. "We don't have any children!" I had gone too far again, but I recovered. "I know, my dear," I said. "But we always *wanted* children, *remember?*"

Mrs. Zok was sad now. "Yes, Herman, I remember. But we didn't know what to do."

"*I* knew what to do," I said. " *I* knew what to do, *Emily.*" I was enjoying myself now.

"Emma!" Mrs. Zok said sharply. "Who's *Emily????*"

"No one," I said. "No one. Only the bag girl down at the A & P. She had big tits." Christ, I thought, what am I doing? I'm getting into a crazy routine with a poor woman who wants to talk to her dear departed husband. I switched to my Norman Vincent Peale manner. "You had a question, dear Emma, what was it?"

"Oh," Mrs. Zok said, "I was just wondering, Herman, whatever happened to the keys to the car?"

"The keys to the car," I mumbled to myself. "Oh

yes. I left them in the car—after I ran head-on into that oil truck."

"What oil truck?" Zok was puzzled. "You died from an overdose of *Vitamin C*, but you *never* had a *cold.* I'll say *that* for *Vitamin C!* God bless Linus Pauling!"

"I'm sorry, Emily," I said.

"Emma!"

"Yes, *Emma,* I said. "I get so mixed up, up here in heaven. Everything is so beautiful. You forget . . . "

"Do you ever see God?" Mrs. Zok wanted to know.

"God?" I said.

"Yes, you know—He's in charge."

"Oh, you mean *Charlton!* No, he keeps pretty well to himself. He *has* to. People are always asking him for favors. You know, how's the Stock Market gonna be next year—and all that kind of stuff." I was beginning to have enough of this seance. And Mrs. Ogelvie was starting to melt a little. Her nose and chin were dripping. We had placed one candle too close to her, and she was starting to drip it out.

"I would like to suggest something," I said, still in Mrs. Ogelvie's imitation voice. "Mrs. Ogelvie is getting tired. I suggest you all retire to the living room where Mrs. Douglas will serve tea, and Mrs. Ogelvie will rest a while."

The Old New Litchridge Occult and Bridge Club wasn't too happy with this, but they got up and turned to the living room just as Mrs. Ogelvie suddenly tilted forward and snuffed out the candle with her nose.

While the Old New Litchridge Occult and Bridge group were milling around our living room, waiting

205

for tea and dainty little cakes (they hoped), Reiko and I worked like Egyptian slaves building the last great Pyramid at Giza.

We stripped Mrs. Ogelvie of her muu-muu, which by this time had adhered to her frozen bulk in many places. We finally had to scissor it off, ruining a good muu-muu but saving a lot of time. We popped her back into her deep freeze just as Herb Hagedorn's wife popped into view. She wanted a shot of Chivas Regal, straight, and to hell with the tea and cakes routine. We were glad to oblige her, and Reiko and I silently thanked God and Buddha that her timing and ours had been just right.

"Help yourself," I said to Mabel (Herb's wife). "You know where it is."

"I should," Mabel said.

Yeah, I thought, and I hope you enjoy your stay at Silver Hill (an expensive drying-out sanitarium nearby, which was loaded with celebrity alcoholics). I felt sorry for the residents of this sanctuary, mainly because it cost $1500 per week.

There was a rumor going around town that Freddie Laker was going to open a "no frills" sanitarium next door to Silver Hill. The "no frills" being all the booze you can drink, but *no television.*

Just a rumor.

CHAPTER

34

THE mystery of what happened to Chief Slocum of the Old New Litchridge Police was finally solved. He had been searching through the Old New Litchridge garbage dump for a tire that he could have recapped for his 1913 Ford Runabout. The Chief was an antique car fanatic, and for years he had been trying to find this particular tire—and maybe a wheel. He had had this 1913 three-wheeled Ford for years and was desperate to find a fourth wheel even if it meant combing the entire dump, which had been created long before 1913. The cause of his untimely death was simple—he had tripped over an old bicycle and landed on a discarded mattress, complete with rusty, broken box spings, one of which, ice-pick sharp, had been sticking up through the moldy ticking like a deadly booby trap.

He should have alerted someone he was going to explore the old dump. It wasn't a safe place to wander over by yourself, as he had proved.

"Poor guy," Reiko said, "he *really* must have *loved* that *old car.*"

"Yeah," I agreed. "Did you ever see his *wife?*"

The baby had now started teething like there was no tomorrow. All night long he cried and fretted and cried and fretted, and gradually toward morning he was crying more than he was fretting and we called Doctor Rosemont. Doctor Rosemont was sleepy but tolerant.

"He's *teething!* It's natural! All babies teethe!" the doctor said.

"All night long?" I wanted to know.

"All night and sometimes for months. Haven't you got a Doctor Spock book there?"

"Yeah, but I thought you being his doctor and all, you should be the first to know."

"Okay, okay," Doctor Rosemont said. "Tell you what you do. You got any Anbesol?"

"You mean that stuff you put on after you get stung by a bee—or a wasp—or a yellow jacket—or a . . . "

"Don't go through the whole list," Doctor Rosemont said. "Just rub a little of that stuff on his gums and call me in the morning."

"It *is* morning," I said. The doctor mumbled something about *why* hadn't he studied law, or philosophy, or herpetology and hung up.

Reiko took a good fifteen minutes taking everything out of our cavernous medicine cabinet and finally found a small bottle of Anbesol. When we rubbed it onto the baby's gums, he made a startled face like we had just given him an Elmer's Glue Oreo, but he stopped crying. I thought he was going to stop breathing, but he didn't.

* * *

208

We got a letter in this morning's mail which puzzled us to say the least. Everything was spelled out in letters clipped from newspapers. It was a ransom note. Why the hell would they be sending *me* a ransom note? For a very good (if you look at it this way) reason. Someone, during the night, had stolen our little gangster, and if we wanted him back we'd have to leave thirty-five dollars (in small bills) in a phone booth at the Texaco station at the corner of Main and Elm before ten o'clock the following night.

"This is kids' stuff," I said. "One of those kids who hang around town."

"What a piece of luck," Reiko said. "That takes care of one part of our problem."

Sure enough, the freezer which had held the little hood was empty. I checked Mrs. Ogelvie's cooler and she was still there, resting comfortably.

"Why couldn't they have taken both of them?" Reiko said.

"God Almighty," I said. "The New York Giants couldn't have taken *both* of them."

"I hope they don't bring him back if we don't pay them the thirty-five dollars."

"There's another way to look at it," I said. "Wouldn't it be a good idea to pay them the thirty-five dollars if they keep him?"

"No," Reiko said. "You can't trust people anymore—not even kidnappers. We'd pay them the thirty-five dollars and they'd bring him back anyway."

We didn't drop the thirty-five dollars off at the Texaco station at the designated time, and immediately, it seemed, we got a phone call.

"What *happened?*" a guarded voice said. "I waited almost an *hour!*"

"Tough," I said.

"What's *that* mean?" the guarded voice wanted to know.

"It means—*no soap!*"

"Hold it," the guarded voice said.

Then it seemed like I could hear a muffled conversation in the background.

Then a not-so-guarded voice said, "Thirty?"

"Nope," I said, feeling very good about at last being in the driver's seat.

"Jesus Christ!" the voice said. "What are you, some kinda fanatic?"

"Yeah."

"You don't want Beansie back?"

"Beansie?"

"Yeah, Beansie Bensonhurst. He's wanted by the FBI, the CIA, the IRS. There's a one hundred dollar reward for him."

"Why don't *you* turn him in and collect the hundred dollar reward?" I asked.

"I can't," the voice said. "There's a *two* hundred dollar reward on *me*."

"Oh," I said. "Well, I wish I could help you out, but I'd rather not call too much attention to myself, at this particular time."

"You *hot?*"

"Er . . . I'm *warming up.*"

"Gosh," the voice said. "This leaves me in a helluva awkward position. If he isn't worth thirty-five bucks . . . "

210

"How about the Old New Litchridge dump. It's the 'in' place for stiffs."

"Yeah," the voice said, "yeah, and thanks." The phone clicked off.

CHAPTER

35

AS a precaution, after the kidnapping of our little stiff gangster, we had Mrs. Ogelvie's deep freeze welded shut again. It wasn't that we were afraid that someone would kidnap her, but they might bring her back—melted.

The baby was still teething loudly. Nightly. And Herb Hagedorn was complaining on the hour, every hour, about being disturbed all night with the baby's crying, and I was beginning to wonder if Herb would fit nicely into our now empty No. 2 deep freeze. One night he complained so much I sneaked out to his driveway and let the air out of his *left front* tire and his *rear right* tire and enjoyed myself very much in the morning when he discovered the flat front tire, got his jack and all his tools out, removed the flat and replaced it with his spare, got into his car and started to drive off when he discovered his right rear tire was flat. I thought he would have a stroke right then and there, but he didn't—he merely took his jack and smashed his shatterproof windshield to bits. Then he went into the house, came out with a full bottle of gin, and lay down in his hammock, and stayed there all day. All night, too.

That night Reiko and I had a serious talk. We knew that sooner or later Mrs. Ogelvie's ratty little nephew would be back with the information that his Aunt Gladys was nowhere to be found. What would we tell him *this* time? The Avon lady had discovered Mrs. Ogelvie's knitting bag (which she was never without) on our coffee table. We knew *this* was no longer a well-kept secret. We managed to get rid of Mrs. Ogelvie's gift from us, the ten-speed racing bike, by the simple expedient of taking it to New York and parking it up against a bench in Central Park. It was stolen in seven minutes, which wasn't even a record.

All of the neighbors had become aware that Mrs. Ogelvie hadn't been seen in quite some time. Mr. Higby, the druggist, knew she was gone. When I gave him his Colt .45 automatic back, he sniffed it to see if it had been fired.

Also we heard rumors that the police had had some very anonymous phone calls about *why* Mrs. Ogelvie's knitting bag had been observed but *she* had *not.*

We knew these calls had come from the Avon Lady, who had been extremely disappointed in our last order. She wouldn't believe that we had a lifetime supply of every Avon product ever made, including a forty-gallon cask of virgin turtle oil, which was guaranteed to tighten your facial muscles or twenty thousand miles, whichever came first.

There were other rumors, none of them reassuring. In fact, all of them made us very nervous. We were ready to break!

213

"Let's go to the police and tell them the whole story," I said.

"Oh boy!" Reiko said.

"I *know!*" I said. " But what is the *alternative?*"

The front door opened, and in walked Mrs. Ogelvie's nephew, Clyde.

"Hello, Clyde," Reiko said. "Your Aunt Gladys is dead."

CHAPTER

36

"THIS is *very interesting*," Sergeant Schwarmer of the Old New Litchridge Police Department said, lighting his malodorous meerschaum for the thirty-first time (I don't know whether he used wet matches or a damp pipe, but it never stayed lighted for more than forty-six seconds) after I had told him the unusual circumstances surrounding Mrs. Ogelvie's death.

"You really think so, Sergeant Schwarmer?" I said, anxious to please.

"Yes. Since Charlie Slocum passed away, it might make *me* the *new Chief*. It's between me and Louie Pagano. Louie's got seniority on me, but this homicide might just give me the edge."

"Homicide!" I yelled. "It's nothing like that. Somebody slipped in the bathtub. It happens all the time!"

"*That's* not gonna make me *Chief*," Sergeant Schwarmer said, reasonably.

"Don't you think maybe you ought to go out and take a look?" I suggested, as things seemed to be grinding to a halt and Sergeant Schwarmer seemed to be of a mind to sit at his desk and just light matches and work on his pipe for the rest of his life.

"Good idea, Douglas," the sergeant said warmly. "Say, you ever done any police work?"

Immediately the liar-writer or writer-liar syndrome hit me. "I was with the Yard for over ten years." I said.

"That's very interesting," the sergeant said. I'm sure he didn't know whether I meant Scotland Yard or our own little back yard with the dead tomato plants up on Heigh-ho Road, but he *did* get up out of his lounge chair and slip into his sergeant's coat with its fifteen medals for off-duty bravery.

The welder, Virgil, took over two hours to get to what used to be our heavenly bower on Heigh-ho Road, and when he got there, we wished he *hadn't*. He was super-abundantly *drunk!* He explained (we think) that it was his birthday and we had just interrupted him, barbecuing and guzzling, at a friendly neighborhood barbecue in his honor. The sergeant, who I thought would be in charge, did nothing, so I had to deal with this unwieldy welder.

"Virgil," I said, "I want you to cut this deep freeze open!"

Virgil was astounded. "You mean you're not gonna bury Rover, after all?"

Immediately Sergeant Schwarmer became a minion of the law. "Rover? Who's Rover?"

"Oh, hello there, officer," Virgil mumbled. "I didn't see you standing there."

"*Who—is—Rover????*" Sergeant Schwarmer said, like he was interrogating Rudolf Hess.

"Tell 'im," Virgil said, as he staggered and tripped

216

over his own feet, wiping out the first three shelves of our spice closet.

"Forget it," Reiko said. Reiko had no patience with drunks. "Go out to your truck, get your torch and light it." Reiko did this to the rhythm of "Get your hat and get your coat and leave your troubles on the doorstep" which was part of "The Sunny Side of the Street" by the immortal Sammy Cahn.

Virgil, the welder, almost sobered up at this voice, which he apparently just discovered, and immediately departed to his truck and brought back his torch— stepping on the cat both coming and going.

"Okay! Okay!" Sergeant Schwarmer had run out of wet matches and was getting impatient. "Light your goddamn torch and let's see what's in this box," he said, kicking the freezer and wincing as he realized he had broken all of his right-foot toes.

Virgil, the welder, went right to work on the *wrong* side of the freezer and in no time he had cut the *hinges* off! We should have watched him, but we were having coffee in the kitchen.

"Okay," Virgil, the welder, said, "all finished."

"You didn't *open* it, did you?" Reiko was panicky.

"No, I just took the hinges off."

"Holy Christ!" I said. "It won't open that way. You gotta cut the other side. That's the way a deep freeze opens, not on the hinge side.

"Oh," Virgil, the welder, said, "if you're going to tell me what to do after sixteen years experience as a welder, then *you* can *do it yourself!*" He handed me the flaming torch, which was sputtering and fuming, just dying to cut through something.

"Please," I said, "I don't know anything about welding or unwelding. You do it! I'm gonna give you a *bottle* to take home to your birthday party," racking my brain to figure which was the cheapest wine we had in our eight-bottle wine cellar.

"Well," Virgil said, "as long as you apologized." Then he set to cutting through the *other* side of the freezer. This didn't take long. It had been welded and unwelded so many times it was weak.

Now came the *big moment!* All four of us, Reiko, me, Sergeant Schwarmer, and Virgil, lifted the lid off the freezer and placed it carefully on the floor.

"Where's the body?" Sergeant Schwarmer said.

Virgil, the welder, didn't care, but Reiko and I sprang to the deep freeze. There was *nothing inside!* Gladys Ogelvie's two-hundred-pound nude body was *not* in the freezer! There was nothing in the freezer but five white, shiny, enameled walls. It was like she or nothing else had *ever* been there.

Virgil, the welder, giggled, gathered up his junk, and careened wildly out our driveway, taking four little apple trees and our mailbox back to his birthday barbecue.

Sergeant Schwarmer borrowed some dry matches, mumbled something about "city folks" and left.

Reiko went upstairs to check on the baby, and I headed for the television set and *The Untouchables* or whatever would help me forget the last few unexplainable minutes.

I heard a *shriek!* I don't think my feet touched any of the steps getting up to the baby's room and Reiko.

Reiko's face was chalk white. "The baby, he's gone!"

CHAPTER

37

SEVENTEEN years have passed since Mrs. Ogelvie disappeared from our deep freezer and our lives— seventeen years since we saw the last of our precious little nameless baby.

Reiko and I sat on the couch in front of the fireplace. Outside the wind moaned to itself, and snow cobwebbed the corners of our picture window. Reiko and I said nothing as we held each other close. There was nothing to say. We just sat and watched the dying fire.

I knew she was remembering. And so was I. It was so long ago, but it was like yesterday—that horrible, agonizing moment.

"I guess," Reiko said, "I guess we'll always wonder whatever . . . "

"We agreed we'd never talk about it again."

"I know."

"Hey," Timothy, our youngest, yelled from the kitchen, where he was stuffing himself with Twinkies, "it's almost time for Lawrence Welk. Put the set on, will you, Mommie?"

Mommie put the set on (very softly) and the telephone rang.

"I'll get it!" Bobby, now sixteen, yelled from his room.

Timothy, his face smeared with chocolate and other ingredients, slammed into the living room and turned Lawrence Welk up to his most saccharin loudness.

Bobby came downstairs. *He* liked Lawrence Welk, too.

"Who was on the phone?" Reiko wanted to know.

"Oh, I dunno—some old lady."

"What do you mean—some old lady?" I said. "What'd she want?"

She didn't want *anything!*" Bobby said, impatient that his attention was being diverted.

"She must have wanted *something!*" Reiko said heatedly. "What did she say?"

"She just said, '*He took almost a whole bottle tonight,*' and hung up . . . and that's *all* I *know!*"